D1328657

Dylan Thomas:
Portrait of a Friend

Gwen Watkins

y Lolfa

First published: 1983
This new edition: 2005

Published with the support of the Welsh Books Council

ISBN: 0 86243 780 6

Published and printed in Wales by
Y Lolfa Cyf., Talybont, Ceredigion SY24 5AP
e-mail ylolfa@ylolfa.com
website www.ylolfa.com
tel. (01970) 832 304
fax 832 782

Contents

Pencil drawing of Vernon Watkins by Alfred Janes

Preface to the new edition

I WROTE THIS BOOK fifteen years after the death of Vernon Watkins. My children had grown up, and I had had time to sort out the masses of papers he left and to separate from the main pile those which related to Dylan Thomas. It appeared to me that he had intended to write a book about his great friend and fellow-poet; and although that book would never be written, I thought that, by putting together some of Vernon's writings and my own recollections of Dylan with what I remembered of Vernon's conversations about him, I could make a book which would be of interest to any reader who wished to know more about the friendship of the two poets and about their poetry.

Most of the critics thought I was wrong. They thought a widow's reminiscences of her husband and his friend, however famous, would not be of great interest, and the book was tepidly reviewed, although not with the vituperation with which *Dylan Thomas: Letters to Vernon Watkins* was received on its publication. No critic actually slated the book, and it sold slowly, until the edition was exhausted, by which time Dylan Thomas had become a world icon, and more and more books were being written about him; and, in consequence, both the *Letters* and *Portrait of a Friend* became primary source books, since there was information in both books that could be found nowhere else. Now, copies can be found, only rarely, in the second-hand book market, and are fairly expensive. What luck it is for any author, to be able to rewrite a book written thirty years before; to correct all the errors that escaped the copy-editor; to show the critics who made unwarranted assumptions where they went wrong; and, best of all, to wipe out every half-baked assumption, every bit of coloured prose, every hypothesis now known to be mistaken; in short, to show that thirty years have made a difference in wisdom, judgment and style – what a gift! Thirty years *must* make a difference, mustn't they?

The best reason for re-issuing the book, however, is that no-one has ever written so well about Dylan Thomas as Vernon Watkins. The unsigned obituary he wrote for the *Times* is now rightly regarded as masterly, but, on every other subject to do with Dylan, he puts the case plainly and from his own intimate knowledge. For instance, who has ever so simply confuted the argument that Dylan's poetry was deliberately obscure? What Vernon said was, "Had he trusted obscurity, he could have been much more obscure, and had he trusted the exploitation of language alone, the body of his finished poetry would have been much greater than it is."

On his broadcast talks: "Dylan Thomas, as a broadcaster, was unique. His place in sound radio was equivalent to Chaplin's place in the silent film. The depth and range of these talks is extraordinary; and extraordinary in its depth and subtle variation was the voice which gave them life."

On the behaviour which seemed at odds with his serious poetry: "He was a poet of tragic vision, but he was also a born clown, always falling naturally into situations which became ludicrous. Just as it is impossible to understand Lear without his Fool, it is impossible to have a clear picture of Dylan Thomas without the self-parody of *Adventures in the Skin Trade*. His infectious humour deceived everyone but himself. The public figure and the lyric poet, whose work began and ended in the Garden of Eden, came to terms, terms which no critic or friend has the complete equipment to analyse."

All lovers of the truth about Dylan should be immensely grateful to the publisher who keeps writing of this stature in the public domain.

Gwen Watkins, 2005

Foreword

No one has written a formal biography of Vernon Watkins, that other Swansea poet, but there are more ways than one of penetrating the past, not least by having been there yourself. Gwen Watkins saw poetry (and two poets) at work from close quarters, and her insights into their lives and labours – men so intimate in some ways, so far apart in others – sound remarkably like the truth.

Her perceptions have been grist to more than one biographer's mill: to mine, certainly. I first approached her many years ago, when I was nudged into doing a Life of the most over-biographied poet of our times, Vernon's (and my) fellow-townsman, the roaring boy of Cwmdonkin Drive. She might have said (and for all I know, she may have thought), Not *another* book about Dylan; why not one about Vernon for a change? But she talked, made sense of many things, nailed memory to the page. She has gone on talking to us literary hacks, only occasionally expressing outrage (accompanied by laughter) at some egregious blunder that caught her eye when she saw the finished product.

In the meantime, she wrote her own version of the story, first published in the 1980s. At the time, I remarked in the *Observer* that 'She looks at both men with an angry candour that makes this by far the best personal memoir of Dylan Thomas in the thirty years since his death.' It is now more than fifty years, and my view hasn't changed. But I emphasise here what I said clumsily then, that the book's strength is that it stands as a memoir to them both, a true story of Thomas and Watkins (even if that makes them sound like a firm of South Wales drapers, long extinct).

This revised version brings the same clear vision, the same sense of delight in the material: whether it concerns the writing of poetry, or Caitlin Thomas pelting her husband with plums, or (before Gwen's time) innocent Vernon and the Thomases spending the night together in the same bed at Laugharne, where nothing happened except giggles from Caitlin.

Some of the time, Gwen is describing what she saw for herself. She met Vernon during the war, when they were both RAF sergeants at Bletchley Park, where the Enigma teams cracked the German codes, and she married him the following year. So from then on, she knew Dylan and Caitlin. But she also heard tales of her husband's earlier friendship with Dylan, from its beginnings in 1935, when Vernon, bank clerk and secret poet, was irritated to see a book called *18 Poems* in a Swansea bookshop, and to discover that he had a rival, eight years younger, who had actually got into print. Gwen also had the drafts and notes that Vernon left behind when he died (playing tennis in Seattle), material that undoubtedly he would have used for a book about his friend had he, too, not succumbed before his time – though he reached sixty-one, against Dylan's thirty-nine.

The relationship was exploited by Dylan, as were all his relationships. But Gwen rejects the idea that her husband was the dreamer with a salary from Lloyds Bank, unable to resist a ruthless beggar and his breezy thank-yous ('TA for the great pound. I heard it singing in the envelope'). Rather, she says, it was the recognition of Dylan's uniqueness that made her husband so willing to oblige. 'He might alter poems [Vernon's], he might not turn up for a wedding [hers], but Vernon had, once and for all, perceived the immense burden of genius under which [Thomas] lived, and could tolerate any shortcomings in his daily life.' A generous statement, perhaps justified.

Mrs Watkins goes on to quote the poem that Vernon wrote in 1938, 'Portrait of a Friend,' which gives her book its title. Dylan had sent a tough-guy photograph of himself with a crack down the middle –

[...] The superhuman, crowned
Saints must enter this drowned
Tide-race of the mind
To guess or understand
The face of this cracked prophet [...]

There was, as she implies, a thread of scepticism in Vernon Watkins' approach to his friend, as there is a (welcome) thread of it in her approach to many things.

But her essential task is to make visible the unseen and forgotten. The evening of Dylan's twenty-second birthday in October 1936, he and Vernon went on a Swansea pub-crawl, starting at the Bay View (today, inexplicably, the Baye View), then proceeding west to Oystermouth and the Mermaid, taking turns to ride Vernon's bicycle. This is now the 'Mumbles Mile,' famous for its fun-loving late-night drinkers and the vomit in the doorways.

Vernon wrote a long poem, 'Sailors on the Moving Land,' about their outing. Like all poems it exists in its own space, but a commentary can help. Emerging tipsy ('The bitter mermaid sang her worst. / Neither throat could slake its thirst'), the poets stagger up the hill, past Oystermouth Castle, taking turns to push the bike.

The moon is shining. Dylan sees the shadow of the other's head with horns growing out of it, i.e. the handlebars, and is terrified at the thought that he is walking with the devil. One is tempted to see this as the self-dramatising nonsense that appealed to Thomas. Yet the poem thinks otherwise. It catches the mood, seizes the moment – 'Edge of the darkness' knife, confessions of despair...'

Remembered scenes are sometimes best conveyed by an observer who was not entirely at ease in the past, who watched in silence; attentive. Gwen watched the intemperate Caitlin – 'always the incarnation of suppressed rage,' as anxious to hurt as Dylan was to placate. She watched Vernon in distress when his second book, *The Lamp and the Veil*, appeared in 1945, and he waited despairingly for a word from his friend, 'the critic for whom [he] cared most,' the man he loved 'unconditionally.' He waited in vain.

At the house near Pennard, on the cliffs beyond Swansea where Gwen and Vernon now lived, Gwen saw Dylan for the last time in 1950, three years before he died. Her long account of the summer day – the 'Swansea gang' of old friends gathered together, the bathing, the foolery, the conversation she had with Dylan when they were alone together for a while – is understated and exact: a scene from an unwritten biography. Gwen Watkins is a survivor we can be grateful for. And her book is a reminder that a Vernon Watkins revival is long overdue.

© **Paul Ferris**, 2005

Acknowledgements

Many of the people who helped me are now dead, but my gratitude to them still lives. Dorothy Fox, OBE, Vernon's sister, and Eric Falk, his lifelong friend, told me many stories of Dylan and Vernon in the earliest years of their friendship. Francis Dufau-Labeyrie, another friend of a lifetime, made available to me, and allowed me to quote from, the whole of the invaluable correspondence between Vernon and himself; and assisted me, besides, with information that I should have found it impossible to obtain from any other source.

The following allowed me to quote from their letters: Caitlin Thomas, Robert Hivnor, Georges-Albert Astre, John Berryman, David Higham Associates Ltd., Charles Monteith and Peter du Sautoy of Faber and Faber, and Lady Snow. Frances Richards gave me permission quote from Ceri Richards's letters. Still living, I am happy to say, are J. C. Wyn Lewis, who gave me a detailed account of Dylan's visit to Cambridge; and Barbara Holdridge of Caedmon Records.

Acknowledgements must also be made to: J. M. Dent and Sons Ltd., and the Trustees of the Copyrights of the Dylan Thomas Estate, for extracts from *Quite Early One Morning* and *The Collected Poems of Dylan Thomas;* to the above and the late Constantine FitzGibbon for extracts from *The Life of Dylan Thomas,* to the above and Faber and Faber Ltd., for extracts from *Dylan Thomas: Letters to Vernon Watkins;* to J. M. Dent and Sons Ltd. and the late Dr Daniel Jones, for extracts from *My Friend Dylan Thomas;* to Hodder and Stoughton Ltd. and Paul Ferris, for extracts from *Dylan Thomas;* to J. M. Dent and Sons Ltd. and the late John Malcolm Brinnin, for extracts from *Dylan Thomas in America*; the late Dr B. W. Murphy, for extracts from *Creation and Destruction: Notes on Dylan Thomas;* and to Sandro Mario Rosso, Editore Stampatore, in Biella, and the late Roberto Sanesi, for an extract from *Taliesin a Gower: Su Una Poesia di Vernon Watkins.*

Material has also been used from the following newspapers and periodicals: *Encounter, Lettres Françaises, Mercure de France, The Mexico City News, The National Review, The New York Times Book Review, The Observer, Poetry (London), Poetry, The Saturday Review, The South Wales Evening Post, The Spectator, Time Magazine, The Times, The Times Literary Supplement, Tribune, Truth* and *The Yorkshire Post.*

Wherever a quotation is used without ascription, it comes from the mass of prose that Vernon Watkins wrote about Dylan Thomas.

"Dylan was so responsive a person where he found affinity in others that the number of biographies which might be written about him would almost equal the number of people he seriously and adequately met. No biography is complete. It is in the collision of these unwritten biographies, when true stories are told, rather than in the distance of popular legend, that the true figure emerges."

Vernon Watkins

Chapter 1

FIRST MEETING

They have put another lunatic into my cell. – D. T.

Not long after noon, on a Monday in February 1935, a young
bank clerk stood in front of the window of Morgan and Higgs'
bookshop in Union Street, Swansea. He should not have been standing
there; he had only an hour for lunch, and it would take him all that
time to order his meal in Lovell's Café, eat it, and run back to Lloyds
Bank in St. Helen's Road. Sometimes, it might take him rather longer,
because, when the harassed waitress at last arrived at his table, he would
say confidingly, "I think I should like it to be a surprise today."

Still, he stood in front of the window, which was filled with books
of poetry – all copies of the same book. A prominent notice announced
'Local Author'. Inside the shop, more copies were piled on a table. The
bank clerk took a few hesitant steps towards the door, then back to the
street, where he stood looking at the window for a little while longer.
('Time yet for a million indecisions.') At last, he went into the shop and,
almost unwillingly, began to look through one of the copies. Finally, he
put it down and hurried out.

He repeated the performance for several days. It was not until Saturday
afternoon, when he left the Bank at about two o'clock, if there had been
no errors in the check-up, that, after more vacillation, he bought the
book and took it home to read.

The bank clerk was Vernon Watkins. He was twenty-seven, and had
been writing poetry since he was seven. He had determined that none of
it should be published until after his death. The book was *18 Poems* by
Dylan Thomas, who was twenty-one; and the best bookshop in Swansea

was full of his first book. Irrationally irritated, Vernon was also, perhaps, irrationally envious. Besides, his mind was completely preoccupied by the poetry of W. B. Yeats, whom he considered the greatest living poet. He did not want to read the poems of any other living poet. He had for years thought himself to be the only poet in Swansea, serving the Muse with utter devotion in the evenings and at the weekends, hearing lines of poetry in his head as he roamed the bays and headlands of Gower. But here was another Swansea poet, so young that the Muse should have had no business with him at all.

Nevertheless, Vernon bought the book and read it. He knew good poetry when he saw it, but still he made no move to meet the poet.

> Then, I ran into his uncle, whom I had known as a child. He said, "You must meet Dylan. His poetry is all modern; but whatever is wrong with his poetry, there's nothing wrong with him."

This uncle was the Reverend David Rees, former minister of the Paraclete, Newton, which was the church that Vernon's father and mother attended when they lived in Caswell Bay, before they moved to Pennard, on the Gower Peninsula. He was said to have told Mrs. Thomas that her son should be in a madhouse; Dylan retaliated by writing a sonnet addressed to his uncle, which began, "I hate you, from your dandruff to your corns."

Perhaps, David Rees thought that meeting Vernon would introduce his nephew to more reputable circles than those he was supposed to frequent when in Swansea. The address that he gave Vernon was, of course, 5 Cwmdonkin Drive.

When Vernon called there, only Dylan's mother was at home. She was to become very much attached to Vernon, and after Dylan's death, she wrote loving letters to him, almost regarding him as a second son; but, on this February day, she was probably anxious and propitiatory. Pre-war Swansea was rigidly class-structured, and she must have had experience of those who thought that D. J. had married beneath him. Vernon's family moved in a different section of its society. His mother came from a county family; his father was an influential bank manager. Vernon and his sisters had been to public schools; he and his elder sister went to Cambridge and Oxford respectively. Mrs. Thomas must have been nervous about the meeting arranged by her brother-in-law.

She need have had no fear that Vernon would be a snob. It was not that he ignored social differences, but that he did not realise that they were there to ignore. He treated charwomen and dukes' daughters with the same, rather shy, courtesy; he could, on rare occasions, be as blazingly indignant with an Air Commodore as with an Aircraftman.

Mrs. Thomas said that Dylan was in London but would get in touch soon after his return. He did, in fact, telephone Vernon the day after his arrival, and they arranged to meet in Pennard, the village on the south Gower coast where Vernon lived with his parents.

> I remember that first meeting very clearly. He was rather shy, but intense and eager in manner, deep-voiced, restless, very humorous, with large, wondering eyes, and under those the face of a cherub. It was a Saturday afternoon, and we went for a walk on the cliffs. We had not gone far when I realised that this cherub took nothing, either in thought or words, for granted, but rather challenged everything with the instinct of a stubborn nature guarding its freshly discovered truth…
>
> I had written a great many poems before we met. On his first visit to me I read him three or four, and when he asked if I had more, he was very much amused when I lugged a trunk into the room. A great many of the poems were derivative in part, for they dated back a long way; but certain ones he liked, and he quickly showed me what was fresh in my work, and what was not.

So began a relationship for which it would be difficult to find a name. On Vernon's side it was like love at first sight, except that love, however idealistic, usually has at least a tinge of the erotic; but Vernon, always fastidiously scrubbed and bathed, admitted with some reluctance that he found Dylan physically "slightly repulsive". I suppose that an intense hero-worship, of the kind Vernon already felt for Yeats, would be the best, though inadequate, description. He loved and admired many poets, living and dead; but the love and admiration he felt for Dylan was passionate and unconditional, and it lasted all his life.

I don't think, however, that the friendship meant as much to Dylan. His friendships, except for those of his childhood, with Daniel Jones, Tom Warner and Fred Janes, were transient; he needed perpetual company, but it did not seem to matter much to him whom he was with. Indeed, as Constantine FitzGibbon points out, he could suddenly become bored with even close friends, and seek other company. He did find in Vernon a devotion to poetry as intense as his own, and this was a novelty and stimulation to him for the first few years of their friendship. This was the first time he had ever been able to read his poetry to a listener who was willing to spend hours discussing a single line or word with intensity equal to that of their author. He had, of course, in return, to listen to Vernon's poems, but this, I think, he did not mind. Poetry of any kind was always interesting to him; he was completely serious when discussing Pamela Hansford Johnson's not very good poems, as he was with the disastrous poems of Margaret Taylor. He liked many of Vernon's poems, and wrote to Oscar Williams, mentioning 'the lovely poems of my friend Vernon Watkins, who certainly should be published in book form in America.' Constantine FitzGibbon heard him read *Portrait of a Friend,* and *Ballad of the Mari Lwyd,* which was no mean feat, as it takes over half an hour; and he sometimes included some Watkins poems in his American readings. But the old, intense discussion of individual poems did not survive Dylan's move from Wales.

There are, also, comparatively few references to Vernon in Dylan's *Collected Letters.* A letter to Glyn Jones, written shortly after the meeting that left Vernon anxious to meet Dylan again as soon as possible, says, "It's very lonely here in Swansea, and the few old friends I have spend their days in work and their evenings in indulging in habits which I've had quite enough of – at least temporarily."

A little later, in a letter to Geoffrey Grigson, Dylan refers to the metre of a German poem he has translated. But he never knew any German, and it is impossible to recognise the metre of a German poem without that knowledge. Vernon must have read the poem to Dylan, explaining both the meaning and the metre; yet there is no reference to him in the letter.

Of Dylan's own letters to Vernon, thirty out of ninety are written to make a straightforward request; for money, for the loan of a suit, for the typing and immediate return of his own poems, for Vernon's help in the criticism or selection of poems for readings. Of the others, a large number describe his poverty, or give news of such occasions as his marriage or the birth of his son, which he knew would elicit a material response from Vernon. At the same time, Dylan's letters are so different from all other letters that I am sure Vernon felt well repaid for any help he may have given. Dylan was also very generous with photographs, with his own first editions and with other anthologies that he was sent and did not want. When he had any money of his own, he was lavish, too, with drinks, meals and hospitality. Critics of Dylan's life often forget this generosity.

He said in one letter that he found Vernon's criticism of his poetry, "…the most helpful there is for me, and I want it to go on." He also said, "I refute your criticism from the bottom of my catarrh," and complained that Vernon's 'ear' was deaf to the logic of his poems. Then again, he begged Vernon to come immediately to Laugharne; "I need you urgently to rewrite a poem with me." But I doubt whether Dylan ever needed anyone in his life to rewrite one of his own poems; he was too confident of his genius for that. It is more likely that he needed money urgently, and knew that the lure of one of his poems would bring Vernon immediately to Laugharne. As John Davenport commented, in a *Spectator* review of Dylan's letters to Vernon, "How brilliant the old boy was at not letting right hands know what left hands were doing!"

When the letters were published, many reviewers made adverse comments about that, and suggested that he would get a kind of spurious kudos from being known to have lent Dylan money. Nothing could be farther from the truth. Vernon's bank salary was small, but he was living at home with his parents, and he had all the necessities and a great many luxuries. Dylan often lacked the bare necessities of life. There was no reason at all why Vernon should not have given Dylan money and other things. He made his point of view very clear in a letter to the *Observer* in 1957:

> I foresaw that lop-sided comment might be made on these small items of borrowing, but I left them in. In their time and context they were significant, mattering so much to him, and not at all to me.

This was certainly true about money; but, sadly, where this relationship was concerned, the reverse was true. All his life, it mattered 'so much' to Vernon, and not at all to Dylan. People were important in Dylan's life only as far as they gave him what he needed. Vernon gave him material help in some ways, he filled in some vacant hours, he did introduce Dylan to some poets he hadn't known (particularly French and German poets) and he did, at least at first, amuse him. He had what Hugo Williams, in the memorial volume, calls 'a zany wit'; strange things happened to him, partly because of his own unawareness of ordinary life; and Dylan was fascinated by his accounts of the cockeyed events that were part of Vernon's daily living. But, eventually, he ceased to need what Vernon could supply and had little further use for him. To Vernon, however, Dylan was from the first, and always remained, a central figure in his life.

Chapter 2

AFFINITIES AND SEPARATIONS

I did not expect, when I turned the pages of this book, that I should find in their author an affinity so much deeper than anything I can describe. – V. W.

The similarities and differences in the lives of Dylan Thomas and Vernon Watkins make a curious pattern. Both spent all the remembered years of their childhood in Swansea. Vernon came there from Maesteg when he was six; three years later, Dylan was born there. They lived on different sides of the Uplands; Vernon to the south of Walter Road, in Eaton Crescent; Dylan to the north, in Cwmdonkin Drive. Both played over the same ground. In an article in the *Texas Quarterly* in 1961, Vernon wrote:

> The grass of the recreation ground can never compete with the boots that play on it. Brynmill Park, offering the olive leaf to doves and foxes, still holds its collection of incongruous cages. Cwmdonkin Park is as it was when Dylan Thomas wrote his poems. It has changed little, since I, too, played in it as a child. The lake of Singleton survives, undisturbed, the activities of builders. St. Helen's cricket ground is greener than ever. There are more policemen, but walls are still climbed, and although hoardings now hinder the spectators from the railway bridge, cricket matches are watched from houses with vulnerable windows, and the latest score seen from the tops of buses and carried round the coast.

Both children went to kindergarten in the Uplands; Vernon to St. Anne's, in Gwydr Crescent; Dylan to Mrs. Hole's, in Mirador Crescent.

Dylan was the naughtiest boy in his class, Vernon the prize scholar who sat at a special desk studying Latin and covering himself with ink. Both schools gave little entertainments at the end of term, in which Dylan and Vernon took part. The child was very much father to the man in these performances. Dylan played to the gallery; instead of acting as the sedate colonel he was cast as, he blew orange peel through the newspaper he was supposed to be quietly reading, and rushed about the stage, beating the air with his walking-stick, until the curtain came down. Vernon, taking part in a Dance of All Nations, missed his cue, and performed his anxiously-rehearsed Irish Jig to the mournful strains of an Indian dirge. The flautist could not see the stage, and Vernon, in mid-stage, could not be pulled off by the eager hands outstretched from the wings. In both cases, the entertainment was disrupted.

The two boys spent their Saturday afternoons in the Uplands cinema, known as the Itch-pit. In a broadcast called *The Place and the Poem*, Vernon spoke lovingly of it.

> In the old days, it used to be protected by a railing, which seemed to have been built specially to keep the Saturday mob at bay. It was the time of the silent film, and the chief excitement every week was the serial, the short, horrifying serial, the serial which left every boy and girl gasping and yet hilarious when the words 'to be continued' flashed upon a situation which knew of no continuation. At that moment, the villain always had the upper hand. The walls of his trap-door dungeon were closing upon our hero and heroine, or knives were coming out of the walls all round them, leaving one space for the final knife to come, or they were on fire, or drowning in water that was gradually filling their cell. Logically, they would die, and the funeral would be on Monday. Illogically, they always just survived, and, on the following Saturday, we hailed their unexplained, hairbreadth escape.

Dylan wrote:

> Week after week, for years and years, we had sat on the edges
> of the seats there, in the dank but snug, flickering dark, first
> with toffees and monkey-nuts that crackled for the dumb guns,
> and then with cigarettes, a cheap special kind that would make
> a fire-swallower cough up the cinders of his heart.

When he was ten, Vernon went for a year to the Grammar School,
where Dylan was to pick up, for a few years, such education as he had.
After that year, Vernon went away to preparatory school in England, but
to him, as to Dylan, Swansea was always his heart's home, the immortal
'ugly, lovely town.'

He recalled:

> When I was away from Swansea... Dylan Thomas brought me
> home to it in a broadcast. It was near Christmas time, and he
> made all the streets come to life. It was as though he had pulled
> a cracker which contained a hat or a puzzle for everyone in
> the town.

Salzburg-on-the-Tawe is what Vernon called it. "Never was there
such a town as ours," wrote Dylan.

Both of them began to write poetry when they were children, and
their descriptions of these early events show, given the differences of
temperament, a remarkable similarity.

D T: ...when I was very young, and just at school, in my eleventh
year, I read indiscriminately, and with my eyes hanging out.

V W: By the time I was ten I had collected most of the English poets.
The hold which poetry had on my sensibility increased, and it
hardly ever relaxed its grip.

D T: I tumbled for words at once... out of them, out of their own
being, came love and terror and pity and pain and wonder.

V W: Words in cadenced form, whether in rhyme or not, seemed to
have an unrivalled power over the imagination. I was deeply

moved by poetry, moved, I mean, to inexplicable tears by a pattern of words which seemed to me unforgettable.

D T: I wrote endless imitations, though I never thought them to be imitations, but rather wonderfully original things, like eggs laid by tigers.

V W: I wrote poems, and they usually reflected the style of the poet I was reading at the time. In language I was not at all precocious, only responsive. It made me confuse my own emotions with those of other poets, and write like them, only very much worse.

D T: When I began to read... verses and ballads, I knew that I had discovered the most important things, to me, that could be ever... I knew, in fact, that I must be a writer of words, and nothing else.

V W: I cannot remember a time when I did not mean to write poetry.

It is not surprising that, with this shared background, there should have been some affinity in their writing.

We were drawn together, partly because we were Welsh, partly because we were both religious poets, partly because we felt that a poem should be serious, and that a good poem was one which could never be fashionable. We particularly disliked *clever* poems, the kind of poem in which a poet seems to say under his breath, "How clever I was to find that way of putting it." We both thought that the rewards in poetry came to the poet when he was most receptive and dedicated, when his imagination was purged of everything but the humility and honesty of its real task, and we both knew that the labour and patience which waited upon those rewards belonged to a unique discipline.

'... we were both religious poets...' This calm assumption entirely ignores the pitched battles of critics and biographers; from Aneirin Talfan's claim that Dylan might have become a Roman Catholic if he had lived, to

Paul Ferris's remark, that religion was merely a stage-prop of his poetry. Vernon and Dylan both loved the great religious poets: Herbert, Milton and Donne, but I doubt whether they ever discussed their own personal beliefs. This would have been difficult, anyway, since neither of them cared for argument, and both were bored by abstract discussion. Dylan would rapidly change the subject, and Vernon had a talent, as Fred Janes said, for always hitting the nail straight on the point.

Vernon later came to believe that Dylan was, if a Christian, rather an unorthodox one. His note to Constantine FitzGibbon, after having read the manuscript of his life of the poet, is probably as good a statement as any of what he thought about Dylan's religious beliefs:

> If he was, as I believe, religious and a Christian, he doesn't need my advocacy, and, if he wasn't, he doesn't want it. Dylan recognised a great error in the past...

In my opinion, he was right to call Dylan a religious poet. One cannot read the late poems without realising that they are full of perception of the numinous, even of the spiritual. After all, the Author's Note to *The Collected Poems* plainly states that, 'These poems are written for the love of Man and in praise of God.'

Yet, Vernon also recognised that, whatever their affinity of theme and attitude, there was a radical difference in the poems they produced.

> I recognised in Dylan Thomas a genius of a quite different kind, which could do with words everything I couldn't do; his writing was, I understood from the first, the exact complement of mine. I disliked every imitation of his work, but his own work I loved, for its unique mastery of texture. Like Hopkins, he always seemed to me a poet whom it was fatal to copy.

Whenever Dylan was in Swansea, or at his parents' home in Bishopston, he and Vernon used to meet, usually to write or discuss poems. When they met at Vernon's home in Pennard, Dylan would sometimes be drawn into Vernon's usual pursuits; they took long windy walks, scrambled over the rocks, went bathing, or rather, Vernon bathed, while Dylan sat and smoked, before coming back to Heatherslade to tea or supper, after which, they played croquet or, in winter, *Lexicon,* the forerunner of *Scrabble.* Although Dylan had been fairly active in his early years, by 1936, walks were already 'unwonted' for him; and as for bathing, Paul Ferris says that, "He never seems to have gone in it (the sea)... on the Gower beaches where he went with friends as soon as he was old enough."

But he did once bathe with Vernon, and in the dark, in October. Sometimes, he would throw stones into the water while Vernon swam. Dylan was amused at his new role, and called himself, 'Your hearty, Britain-chested, cliff-striding companion.' At the Heatherslade meals, he was, according to Eric Falk, Vernon's lifelong friend, a model guest, drinking tea or home-made lemonade, liking a glass of water by his side, to sip at during card games, always polite and pleasant to Vernon's parents and their guests. Occasionally, he would invite Vernon to tea at Cwmdonkin Drive, and the same decorous scenes were enacted.

Dylan did not, in these early days, make any attempt to draw Vernon into his world of pubs and dives. A letter of December 1935 says, "I live a comfortable, sheltered, and now only occasionally boozy life in Swansea..."

They would sometimes have a drink after Vernon left the Bank, and then go back to Cwmdonkin Drive, to spend the evening on their poems.

"The poetry machine," Dylan continues in the same letter, "is so well oiled now that it should continue without a hitch until my next intellectually ruinous visit to the bowels of London."

Later, during the war and after, when it became impossible to see Dylan unless you went to a pub, they did habitually meet there; but, in these pre-war days, there is only one record of them both getting drunk together, and that was on Dylan's birthday – a day he could not celebrate without beer. Dylan, however, did his best to make it clear to Vernon that the country life Vernon loved was not for him, except as a pastoral interlude:

...the out-of-doors is very beautiful, but it's a strange country to me, all scenery and landscape, and I'd rather the bound slope of a suburban hill, the Elms, the Acacias, Rookery Nook, Curlew Avenue, to all these miles of green fields and flowery cliffs and dull sea going on and on. I'm not a country man; I stand for, if anything, the aspidistra, the provincial drive, the morning café, the evening pub...

It is strange, then, to think how full his last great poems are of green fields and cliffs and the anything-but-dull sea. Vernon must have been staggered by this near-blasphemy about his beloved Gower, but still it made no difference to the intensity of his feelings.

Dylan may have mistaken the nature of these feelings, or at least have mischievously wanted to test them, since he proposed one week-end that he, Vernon and Caitlin should all sleep in one bed. This was the first weekend that Vernon stayed with the married couple in Laugharne. They were then living in Gosport Street, in the 'small, damp fisherman's furnished cottage', found for them by Richard Hughes; and the double bed, referred to by Dylan in a letter to Henry Treece as 'a swing-band with coffin', was to be the scene of the temptation. Dylan had been curious about Vernon's sexual life ever since they had met. In fact, Vernon's days at the Bank were long and his hours with his Muse too short. Romantic feelings he certainly had, but they were for poets and poems. He wrote of one encounter, to Francis Dufau-Labeyrie, the Don Juan of two countries:

At the last sweetshop you would have kissed the maid, a beautiful Welsh girl but I only made her laugh while our lives flew for a moment into a mutual bit of butterscotch. It's no good. I cannot be romantic. I prepare the apple-pie bed for every likely customer, the tin mirror for all bright eyes.

Whether Dylan thought the beautiful Caitlin might tempt him, or whether he thought Repton had left its mark, there is no way of telling;

but he announced that there was only one bed in the cottage, and that it was large enough for them all. Yet, a few weeks later, he was writing to Henry Treece, "There is a double bed in one room, two single beds in the other."

Throughout his life, it never occurred to Vernon to doubt any statement, on any subject other than poetry, as long as it was made with a straight face. Christopher Isherwood describes, in *Lions and Shadows,* how he and 'Chalmers' (Edward Upward) convinced Vernon (in the character of 'Percival') that they had made a new and highly sinister acquaintance:

> The gullible Percival believed this, and was deeply impressed, but when Chalmers, carried away by his own improvisation, went on to describe how Moxon kept a cat in a birdcage and a canary flying free about the room, and when I added that he kept a large black serpent which accompanied him on rambles after dark, Percival began to smile reproachfully, and murmured, in his deep musical tones, "Do you know, I believe you're ragging me?"

So it was not surprising that he accepted with complaisance Dylan's allotment of the available sleeping space, and was only anxious to occupy it as soon as possible. It was the last day of a week's holiday from the Bank, which he had spent cycling in North Wales; he had, he wrote to Francis, "...a sore bottom after doing eighty hilly miles to Laugharne." He had been taken to drinks at the local pub, he had undergone an exhausting introduction to Richard Hughes of Laugharne Castle, and he was more than ready for bed. So, he tumbled gladly into it, and was asleep before Caitlin came upstairs. Unfortunately, he had rolled into the hollow in the centre of the big old mattress, and had to be awakened by a frantic Dylan, who had envisaged Caitlin doing a little tempting from the bedside, but not actually sleeping next to Vernon. Dylan tried to push the much more muscular Vernon to one side, while he himself clambered down into the dip, a feat much more difficult than it sounds, as the sleepy cyclist kept rolling back into it. He remembered vaguely half-waking at intervals, to hear Dylan cursing and groaning, and Caitlin giggling. This incident explains the otherwise cryptic remark in Vernon's letter to Francis about the weekend. "I stayed with Dylan and Caitlin…Caitlin could cook, *wake up* [my italics], sew, clear away, wash up, light fires and do everything I thought she couldn't do."

Whatever Dylan had hoped to find out from the experiment remained undiscovered, and the incident was never referred to again. Vernon remained innocently under the impression that all overnight visitors were entertained by Dylan and Caitlin in this hospitable manner.

'Would you like to go down one weekend with me?' he wrote to a friend. 'We couldn't stay with them, though, as they can only put one person up.'

It was perhaps fortunate that he did not stay in Laugharne again until the Thomases had moved to Sea View, where he slept in the cardboard bed, which he was later to save from repossession by a hire-purchase firm, spending the money he earned from the publication of some poems about his godson, Llewellyn.

After a long breakdown, in his twenty-second year, Vernon had kept his poetry apart from what most people would call his ordinary life. He worked in the Bank every day and wrote poetry every night. He said, without resentment, that no-one in Lloyds had ever shown the slightest interest in his poetry until he was awarded the Guinness prize; then, he said, they were interested in the prize money, not the poem that had won it.

Now, he had met a poet who, while rejecting the world of paid employment, still took that world on its own terms and made his poems part of his daily life and of that world. His friends noticed that Vernon became oddly protective about Dylan, who was not to be criticized, nor to be held accountable for any failure to keep appointments, nor for any other peccadilloes. He was not to be forced, by the opinions of society or financial necessity, to abandon the daring, arduous but romantic life of living on and by words that he had chosen. Did Vernon feel guilty that he had not made this choice? At any rate, the life he had chosen enabled him to subsidise Dylan marginally, and this he gladly and faithfully did. Dylan was a kind of *alter ego,* a poet who had taken the road at which he himself had baulked, or had not been allowed to take.

Vernon, I think, always saw Dylan as the genius who had matured so early in his art, and did not perceive the lack of maturity in the man who wrote to his girl before their marriage:

> Do you look like a real adult person, not at all anymore beautiful and barmy like the proper daughters of God? You mustn't look too grown up, because you'd look older than me; and you'll never, I'll never let you, grow wise, and I'll never, you shall never let me, grow wise, and we'll always be young and unwise together...

This seems, alas, only too accurate a picture of their future. Perhaps Dylan's preference for the free life of the child was partly willed, but there appears to be in his nature a real inability to accept adult responsibility. Perhaps nowadays, he would be diagnosed as having a personality disorder. He did make attempts to look after his wife and children, but they were occasional and inconsistent. He relied, on the whole, on being helped by other people, as a child is helped. But to be childlike is one thing; to be childish when grown up is quite different. Vernon was childlike in many ways; practical life often defeated him, but he could never have been irresponsible in the way that Dylan was. Because he understood, in some ways, what it was to find ordinary life difficult, he was always very protective of Dylan's inability to cope with the responsibilities of adult life.

Their personalities were, in fact, more alike than they appeared. Dylan is thought of as outgoing and talkative, Vernon as reserved and sometimes almost withdrawn, but they were actually both very shy; they simply dealt with this shyness in different ways. They found it difficult to talk unreservedly to each other, or possibly to anyone else, about anything other than poetry; but this difficulty was overcome by the continual use of humour.

Owen Barfield says that:

> In the parameter of conversation between close friends, a
> sustained ebullition of humour can perform two opposite
> functions. It can increase it by enabling intimate allusions which
> would be coarse or indelicate in any other form. But it can also
> arrest the progress of intimacy at a critical juncture, whether
> it comes as the unplanned interruption by a ruling habit, or,
> used of set purpose, is raised like the traffic policeman's hand,
> gentler but not a whit less effective than the red light.

We see this in most of Dylan's correspondence with Vernon. All
references to his extreme poverty are humorous, as are thanks for help; his
disorderly life in London is described comically, even his announcement
of his marriage is funny. The two talked about poetry seriously, they
talked about everything else in their lives humorously or not at all.

In another aspect of their lives they were both alike and very different.
To both of them, words were almost the most important things in life; but
Dylan was satisfied with English words, while Vernon spoke French and
German fluently, and Italian well enough to translate Dante. He knew
enough Latin to translate Virgil and enough Greek to translate Homer.
He always said that when the Muse was proving stubborn about his own
verse, he would turn to translation. He loved French and German poetry,
and could repeat much by heart. Dylan would listen with interest to his
readings of Rilke, Lorca and other foreign poets, but never showed the
faintest interest in learning any language but his own; even when he lived
in Italy for three months, he made no attempt to learn the language, nor
did he show any interest in Italian. Although both men came from pure
Welsh families, whose first language for generations had been Welsh, and
whose parents were Welsh-speaking, neither spoke Welsh; but that was
common in the twenties and thirties, but Vernon did read the old Welsh
poets: Llywarch Hen, Dafydd ap Gwilym and the like, with his father,
and listened to his mother's translations of the Welsh hymns she loved.

Most critics, indeed most people who knew them both, found it easy to see the differences – of feeling, behaviour, attitude, lifestyle, and the kind of verse they wrote – between Vernon and Dylan. It was not so easy to perceive the affinity, the likeness, which Vernon found so deep.

Chapter 3

KARDOMAH DAYS

The richness of the letters I was now re-reading brought back to me, with the atmosphere of pre-war Swansea and Laugharne, a situation, an era and an excitement which cannot be repeated. – V. W.

Vernon's admiration of his new friend had time to turn into hero-worship in the few weeks after their first meeting, before Dylan went to Derbyshire in April to stay with A. J. P. and Margaret Taylor. In Pennard, Vernon had read his own poems to Dylan. On the return visit to Cwmdonkin Drive, the next week, Dylan read his poems, from a folder on which he had printed in large capitals the word POMES. The first poem he read was *Ears in the Turrets Hear*, and then, *Should Lanterns Shine*. He had completed seven of the sonnets in the sequence *Altar-wise By Owl-light in the Halfway House*, and these, too, he read. When he reached the last line of the seventh,

'On rose and icicle the ringing handprint,' there was a moment of silence, and then he looked up. The lamp behind his head made his golden hair into a halo, and the echo of his beautiful voice still trembled in the air. It was a moment which stayed in Vernon's memory all his life. It was no wonder that the combination of poetry, lamplight and young Adonis not yet dead, but already on the way to apotheosis, should heighten Vernon's feeling into something like reverence.

"I was aware," he said, "that I was in the presence of a poet of extraordinary genius."

The whole world had shrunk for him to the compass of that small room,
and nothing that happened later changed his feelings.

Praise God, although a time is gone
That shall not come again,
If ever morning rightly shone,
A glass to make all plain,
The man I mourn can make it live,
Every fallen grain.

I see the house where we would meet;
I see my steps return;
Kicking the sparks of the Swansea street,
And still those windows burn,
Struck by the sunrise hour of life
With all men's lives to learn.

My echoing footsteps when they stop
Reconstitute the town,
That working window at the top,
The neophyte and clown
Setting the reel and arc-light up
To pull illusion down.

Climbing Cwmdonkin's dock-based hill,
I found his lamplit room,
The great light in the forehead
Watching the waters' loom,
Compiling there his doomsday book
Or dictionary of doom.

More times than I can call to mind
I heard him reading there.
His eyes with fervour could make blind
All clocks about a stair
On which the assenting foot divined
The void and clustered air.

That was the centre of the world,
That was the hub of time.
The complex vision faded now,
The simple grew sublime.
There seemed no other valid stair
For wondering feet to climb.

That strictest, lie-disrobing act
Testing the poem read
Which, after toil and plumbing,
Left the first cause unsaid,
Showed me his nature then as now,
The life he gave the dead.

There, near Cwmdonkin, first and last,
Witness of lives below,
He held the unrisen wisdom fast
From heaven in overthrow,
Where lamps of hooded meaning cast
Light on the words below.

After he had finished reading the poems, Dylan asked Vernon if he used
a dictionary. Vernon answered that he occasionally did, but Dylan said,
"No, I mean a real dictionary, like this," and took down from a shelf
a book made of folded sheets of brown paper sewn together. It was
a rhyming dictionary, which he had compiled himself, and to which
he constantly made additions. This, he said, was his Doomsday Book.
He also showed Vernon the manuscript of his story, *The Orchards*. This
was written in his minute, Emily-Brontë-like hand, on the inside of the
cover of a large cardboard box made to hold ladies' blouses. He said that
his mother obtained these boxes for him from an obliging draper, since
he found that it helped him to see a story in its entirety, rather than on
successive pages. (What would one of these box-lids, doubtless thrown
away once the story was published – be worth now?) Dylan read this
story aloud, too. In it appeared for the first time the name Llareggub,
later to become known all over the world. It was from James Joyce, the

prose-writer he most admired at that time, that he had learned this kind of word-play. He displayed, as well, the manuscripts of *The Lemon* and *A Prospect of the Sea*, still in the making, and told Vernon about his friend Tom Warner, to whom the second of these stories was dedicated. Tom was a musician, who had been brought up by two elderly aunts; and once, said Dylan delightedly, when Tom was lying on his bed, wondering anxiously whether he would be able to get a job, or whether he would have to play the trumpet for pennies outside pubs, an aunt had called up to him, "Tom! Tom! *Water the fuchsia!*" ("What of the future?")

Vernon stumbled down the hill, to catch the last bus back to Pennard, dazzled by his new friend's brilliance and exhausted from his day's work in the busy, understaffed St. Helen's Road branch of Lloyds Bank. He was not too exhausted, however, to rush into Wyn Lewis's house and cry, "I have spent the evening with a genius! You must meet him too!"

Wyn lived next door to the Watkins's house, Heatherslade. Wyn and Dylan were born within a month of each other, and both had played in Cwmdonkin Park, members of rival infant gangs. The tots in Wyn's gang were terrorised and rolled in the gravel by the stronger, rougher members of the other gang. At this time, Wyn was a Cambridge undergraduate, home for the Easter vacation.

Vernon pressed a copy of *Eighteen Poems* on Wyn, and disappeared, as Philip Larkin was to describe him on another occasion, 'exalted into the night.' There was time before Dylan left for Derbyshire in April for him to come to tea on one more Saturday at Heatherslade; and, after tea, Vernon took Dylan to Windyridge, to meet Wyn and play croquet.

Wyn and Vernon were fanatical croquet opponents, neither willing to lose and each believing that if he had lost, it was merely a fluke, which could easily be retrieved in the next game. This meant that the next game had to be played immediately, occasionally lasting until after midnight, with torches and a beady-eyed competitor to hold a handkerchief behind the hoop, to make it visible. It was to this serious, cut-throat game that Dylan was to be introduced.

Wyn had read *Eighteen Poems* and was prepared to be awed by genius, but Dylan was shy, and at first talked only to Vernon. When he became more at ease, he was neither exhibitionistic nor flamboyant. He talked politely, made efforts to learn the new game, and seemed interested by it. He was courteous and deferential to Wyn's parents. After supper, he talked a little about the poetry of W. H. Davies, and read one of his poems. Apart from the beauty of his voice, Wyn could see nothing exceptional about him.

After leaving Derbyshire, Dylan went to Ireland, but he was back in Swansea in the autumn. On the 6th of October, he sent Richard Church the manuscripts of most of the poems he had written since *Eighteen Poems*, omitting the still unfinished sonnet-sequence. It was now that Vernon began to see him regularly, as often as two or three evenings a week. He also went on Wednesdays during his lunch hour to the Kardomah café, where he met Alfred Janes, Tom Warner, Charles Fisher, John Prichard and other young men. Daniel Jones was abroad by this time, and Vernon did not meet him until they were both posted to Bletchley Park during the war, but Dylan had talked so much about him that Vernon was able to recognise him immediately, when they did eventually meet.

The Kardomah was actually the old Congregational Church where Dylan's parents had been married. The main body of the church was where most of the customers now sat; in the former gallery, the young men and girls sat and giggled, drinking coffee-dashes and eyeing one another furtively. This was where Dylan and his friends gathered, all young men who were interested in and practised the arts. Dylan and Vernon were poets, John Prichard a writer, Charles Fisher a journalist, Fred Janes a painter, and Tom a musician. They all had very little money; even Vernon and Charles, who had jobs, did not earn very much. For the first time since leaving Repton, Vernon was among men who cared deeply about the arts. He was to remember the Kardomah with affection, long after it had been destroyed in the three-day blitz on Swansea.

> Nobody has rebuilt the Kardomah, where Swansea's rich artists and poverty-stricken businessmen used to meet, on separate floors to discuss shares and pictures. The old shopping centre

of Swansea is a ruin, as big as the Coliseum… I begin to think
that Swansea was once a better place.

He grew very fond of Tom Warner and Fred Janes, and had a fund
of stories about the Kardomah meetings. Once, when his paintings were
being praised, Fred had noticed that the attractive girl at the next table
appeared to be listening. He kicked Dylan furtively, and whispered,
"More of that, *and louder!*"

When other artists' work was being discussed, and he had waited in
vain for a mention of his own name, he had risen from the table, stared
into a mirror on a nearby wall, and sat down again, saying sadly, "*And
handsome, too.*"

When Dylan and Vernon had been talking for too long about poetry,
he would paralyse them by saying sternly, "POEMS IS MUCK!" Or
Tom would tell them of how, when he was at the Grammar School, the
fearsome Latin master announced, one Friday, a test on irregular verbs for
the next Monday. Tom, a timid child, had spent the weekend praying
that something would happen to stop, or at least postpone, the test. When
they arrived at school on Monday, all was confusion; the Latin master
had died suddenly on the Saturday, "And," concluded Tom in a whisper,
"I have never dared to pray since."

Delightful though the Kardomah meetings were, they were not as
precious to Vernon as the evenings he and Dylan spent in Cwmdonkin
Drive, discussing and sometimes revising the poems to go into Dylan's
next book. Richard Church was dubious about their obscurity and their
supposed Surrealistic content. Vernon and Dylan were indignant at this
unwarranted assumption. Vernon was later to point out that, although
there was Surrealist imagery in some of the early stories, the only image in
the whole of Dylan's poetry that could be called Surrealist was in *After the
Funeral*, the image of the slit throat of the boy shedding dry leaves.

About Church's accusation of obscurity, Dylan cared little. Vernon
tried to persuade him to leave out of the book two of the poems: *Now, Say
Nay,* and *How Soon the Servant Sun,* which he was sure the critics would

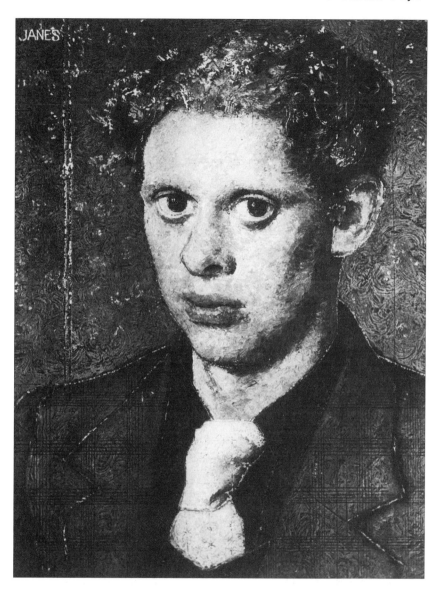

Portrait of Dylan Thomas by Alfred Janes
(Original in the National Museum of Wales, Cardiff)

attack because of their baffling and provocative confusion of meanings.

"Oh, give them a bone," said Dylan carelessly, and added that, as far as he knew, one at least of those poems had 'no meaning whatsoever.'

Vernon did, however, persuade Dylan to include one very well-known poem, *And Death Shall Have No Dominion*. Dylan was not satisfied with it, and had determined to leave it out, but Vernon, after hearing it read again and again, became excited by what he called its 'impulsive rhythm', and began the routine they had devised for the revision of poems. This consisted of reading each line of the poem separately and considering whether there was any word which was not completely satisfactory. If there was, they would throw words at each other, perhaps forty or fifty possible words, which would then be tried in the line. If one of these was accepted, this might change the balance or texture, so that other changes would have to be made. It was an exhaustive and exhausting procedure, but, at the end of the evening, Dylan had made several changes and had agreed that the poem should be included in the new book. I wonder how many lovers of Dylan's poetry, listening to the windy bombastics of this poem, booming out on memorial occasions, have regretted this decision.

A change that was certainly for the better was also due to Vernon. The last two lines of *Should Lanterns Shine,* on its appearance in *New Verse* in December 1935, were:

Regard the moon, it hangs above the lawn;
Regard the lawn, it lies beneath the moon.

These lines seem to have no connection with the rest of the poem, and are, besides, much more like Eliot influenced by LaForgue than like Dylan Thomas. The two previous lines make a much better ending:

The ball I threw while playing in the park
Has not yet reached the ground

All things considered, Dylan was pleased with the poems. He thought them better than those in *Eighteen Poems*. They do, indeed, show a much greater variety of rhythm and stanza form, and even when he felt that one of them, such as *I, In My Intricate Image*, was not entirely successful, he still thought it better than anything he had done up to that time. He was disappointed that Vernon, on hearing this poem for the first time, did not notice the seventy-two concealed rhyme-endings on the letter L.

"I thought you at least would have noticed that," he said reproachfully, and Vernon felt suitably guilty.

Vernon's only criticism of the twenty-five poems was that the lines were too packed with meaning, that there were no 'numb' words and lines to give the poems natural extension. He quoted lines of Yeats in which at least half of the words were 'numb':

> But he calls down a blessing on the blossom of the may,
> Because it comes in beauty, and in beauty blows away.

But that was not Dylan's way. "If my readers want a breather, they won't get one from me," he said. "Let them go away and have a game, then they can come back to my next line."

A poem that Vernon particularly admired was *Then Was My Neophyte*, which was finished about this time. After Dylan died, Vernon often used it in his many readings of Dylan's verse, because he saw it as:

> A prophecy of his own melodramatic death, shown to him on a
> film, which he, as a child whose character has not been formed,
> sees unwinding and projected on a screen… under water.

Vernon was not much of a film-goer, even in the thirties, the great days of the film. One reason for this was that he was completely incapable of following a plot. Kingsley Amis said of him that, when he saw the hero of a film pacing up and down a hospital waiting-room, lighting cigarette after cigarette, his sole deduction was that the chap was a heavy smoker. He did enjoy films in which plot was unimportant, such as those of the Marx Brothers, Chaplin and Laurel and Hardy. But Dylan loved all films. He once told Vernon that really bad films gave him a particular thrill. His own film scripts and his unfinished novel, *Adventures in the Skin Trade* were to show, perhaps, that he was incapable of inventing sustained narrative, but he could follow a plot. After the selection of *Twenty-Five*

Poems was complete, some of the evenings spent in Cwmdonkin Drive and Pennard were spent in reading prose.

Vernon's knowledge of poetry was probably greater than Dylan's, but his experience of prose literature was minimal indeed. He believed that reading prose spoiled the ear for poetry, as playing squash spoiled the hand and eye for tennis. Perhaps he thought prose was merely a kind of failed poetry; at all events, he read nothing but the Bible, especially the poetic books, Job and Ruth, the prose of Yeats, which he considered a kind of poetry, and the works of Kierkegaard, whom he considered as a poet who happened to write in prose.

Dylan, on the other hand, was a voracious reader of prose. He had read Dickens and Joyce, at one end of the scale, and every cheap thriller he could lay his hands on, at the other. It is no wonder that, to Vernon, he seemed 'fabulously well-read.'

This was not D. J. Thomas's opinion. He complained to Vernon, one day at supper, that his son was terribly narrow in his reading.

"Narrow!" exclaimed Dylan. "Why, *he* stops reading when the words go on to the edge of the page!"

Not even Dylan could persuade Vernon to go on reading when the words went on to the end of the page, but he could, and did, read aloud to him. He read Joyce's *Dubliners*, almost his Bible at that time, Djuna Barnes's *Nightwood,* and Caradoc Evans's short stories, and read all the characters in different voices. This was a revelation to Vernon, who, besides being poor at plot, had never really made much of dialogue, either. He was amazed, too, to see how Dylan's 'jackdaw eye' enabled him to pick out from his reading bits and pieces that would one day be fitted into their proper places in poems.

For instance, the Doctor's cry in *Nightwood*, "I tell you, Madame, if one gave birth to a heart on a plate, it would say 'Love', and twitch like the lopped leg of a frog," became, in *After the Funeral*: "The stuffed lung of the fox twitch and cry Love."

One day, while working on 'a poem about churches', Dylan told Vernon that, while reading a boring thriller, he had been transfixed by the words, 'The shadow is dark directly under the candle.' This became the line:

There is loud and dark directly under the dumb flame,

from the poem in *The Map of Love*, beginning:

It is the sinners' dust-tongued bell claps me to churches.

In one of their few late meetings, he told Vernon that he was determined in one of his poems to use the line:

See, see where Christ's blood streams in the firmament!'

But he did not live long enough to write that poem.

Vernon has paid tribute to what Dylan did for him in these meetings. "He showed me what was fresh in my work, and what was derivative."

Dylan, though younger, was a much more mature poet than Vernon, and needed no such help, but he was interested in Vernon's wider and, perhaps more concentrated, reading of verse. Vernon had always been addicted to reading one poet at a time, perhaps for six months or longer; and the poet he had been reading for a long time now was W. B. Yeats, of whom he wrote:

… whom I regarded then and still regard as the greatest lyric poet of our age. I, already in 1935, when I met Dylan Thomas, owed more to Yeats than to any other poet, as he had shown me something which the others had not been able to show, that is, how a lyric poet should grow old. This was certainly something to do with what Yeats himself called, 'the greater sincerity of an artist's life'; but this alone would not have explained his extraordinary capacity for self-renewal; as a poet he was willing, at any age, to dedicate himself completely to his vision, believing always in its miraculous fruit. It was not so much that Yeats grew old impressively, but that, as he aged, his poems grew better and more astoundingly fresh, 'moving', as he said, 'continually, like Swedenborg's angels, towards the dayspring of their youth.'

Dylan, of course, knew all the anthology pieces of Yeats, *The Lake Isle of Innisfree, Aedh Wishes for the Cloths of Heaven, No Second Troy,* but of the great books of the thirties he knew nothing. When he heard the poems in them, he agreed with Vernon that Yeats was 'the greatest by miles.' Still, his own favourite poet remained Hardy; but here again he knew only selections, and it was Vernon who lent him his own *Collected Poems of Thomas Hardy,* which enraptured him. Vernon remembered him laying his hand on the book and saying solemnly, "There is not a single poem in this book that I wish had not been written." It was not that he failed to see the faults in some of the poems, but that he loved the faults too. Vernon thought Hardy a great poet, but, for himself, he knew that he could never write a poem 'dominated by time.'

He was happy, though, to listen to Dylan reading Hardy's poems aloud, especially his favourite, *To Lizbie Brown,* and *An Ancient to Ancients,* to which, he said, *And Death Shall Have No Dominion* was a distant relation. The Hardy poem that Vernon liked best to hear Dylan read was *In Death Divided.*

> I shall rot here with those whom in their day
> You never knew,
> And alien ones who, ere they chilled to clay,
> Met not my view,
> Will in your distant grave-place ever neighbour you.

It was to Hardy that Vernon turned when he heard that Dylan had died in America, before it was known that his body would be brought home to Laugharne. He took down the blue, old-fashioned book that Dylan had handled and read from so often, and, without opening it, he said three lines from the same poem:

> The eternal tie which binds us twain in one
> No eye will see
> Stretching across the miles that sever you from me.

Chapter 4

THE DEMON DRINK

Brandy and ripe in my bright, bass prime... – D. T.

In September 1936, with the publication of *Twenty-Five Poems*, Dylan became an established poet. When Edith Sitwell reviewed it in the *Sunday Times*, he became famous.

He confronted his celebrity as he confronted everything else – with shyness, with showing-off, with pleasure, with indifference, with confidence. He and Vernon always felt some measure of disdain for critics, believing that, whether the poem was successful or not, only the poet knew what it was meant to be, and how much its composition had cost. Vernon was shown dozens of letters, a few from admirers, but many from angry or bewildered readers complaining of the obscurity of the poems. One in particular, from a member of the Athenaeum, enraged Vernon, because the writer sneered at the meaninglessness of lines which he thought among the most beautiful in the book.

"I shan't answer any of the others," said Dylan. "But I might write to him."

"And explain to the fool how long those poems took to write?"

"No. I shall say, Dear member of the Athenaeum, will you meet me on the steps of your club, so that I can knock you down them?"

The month before the Sitwell review came Dylan's twenty-second birthday. Birthdays were, wrote Vernon:

always for him occasions for reflection – some of his finest poems were suggested by them – and for unstinted celebration... The accident that he arrived in America just before his 39th birthday may have assisted that very instinct of generosity which was to prove fatal to him.

On October 27, 1936, Vernon spent the evening of Dylan's birthday with him. They started off with a drink at the Bay View Hotel, then took turns to ride Vernon's bicycle along the Mumbles Road to Oystermouth, ending up at Dylan's favourite pub, the Mermaid. Vernon recorded this occasion in a long poem called *Sailors on the Moving Land*, which was published in *Life and Letters Today* in 1949 – although the first of its many drafts is on pre-war paper, and the last is dated 1956, three years after Dylan's death.

The occasion was a comic one, yet the poem is serious. In drunkenness, inhibitions disappear, and perhaps confidences were made which would not have been made sober; at any rate, Vernon perceived something of the essential tragedy of Dylan's life and personality.

> Before the safety curtain dropped
> Upon all knowledge, while we stopped
> The edge of distance, by degrees
> October brought no flying grains
> Rustling behind the Mumbles trains
> Passing our faces where time stopped,
> Leaving this music of the tunnelled seas.
>
> Dusk before war, and swallows in their crowd
> Whirl in a pointed cloud.
> Now they are gone. What instinct chooses?
> Faced by the Judgment, who is not a cheat?
> What eye now sees, now loses
> His brother's face, a stranger in the street?

They were already tipsy as they threaded their uncertain way along the narrow Oystermouth pavements, past the shops, still, in those pre-war days, open till nine or ten o'clock.

'I have a bicycle that is not mine.'
     'The round moon racing through the clouds is fine.'
'I have seen Lamprey's marble crossed by eels.'
     'Must we be mastered by the moving wheels?'

So to the inner smoke, the quarrelling air,
Angry jolting of a chair,
Edge of the darkness' knife, confessions of despair;

The bitter mermaid sang her worst.
Neither throat could slake its thirst.

Tritons of the sea shed tears,
But you, with terror in your head,
Shook philosophy out of your ears,
Snatched a great light, and said:

'I have a cage of darkness, hiding
The great white innocent bird, the albatross,
And where the waters toss,
This way and that way riding
White horses of the cradle or the fosse,
To wordless islands and the One-Eyed Man,
I know the horrible gulf from which we ran.
Speak, if you know the place where speech began.'

When the pub closed, they were turned out into the street that heaved like the sea under their feet, and started up the hill past Oystermouth Castle, sometimes taking turns to push, or lean over, the bicycle, and sometimes discovering that neither of them was pushing it, so that they had to retrace their steps to find it lying in the gutter. Once, in the bright moonlight, the shadow of Vernon's head appeared to have grown horns (in reality the shadow of the handlebars). Dylan became terrified, insisting that he was walking with the devil, and it was with great difficulty that he was persuaded to go on.

Time. Time. Time. Time.
Thunderbolts of death and birth.
Thunderbolts of rut and rout.
How many from the contemporary tomb

Who had found warmth and comfort here, stepped out
To the stampeding Earth.

So from Oystermouth's nets of Wales
Followed by the fishes' tails
And every print and spoor of grief,
Where the dull trees were lopped of every leaf
We climbed through darkness where you danced about,
Gay as a babbling thief.

Oystermouth Castle floated round
A sea of undulating ground.
Two moon-flung shadows, bent to steal
The navel-stone no man had found,
Zig-zagged uphill, fell flat across the wheel.

Two with a bicycle, two men with horns.
Two shadowed quarrellers pushing two moons.

It took Vernon three hours to cover the seven miles to Pennard. He could never remember where Dylan left him. What he did remember was that he had seen for the first time the profound unhappiness that lived beneath the mask.

And morning, morning, morning followed fleet;
The playing pavings, gathering flying feet,
Hammered the dark of eyelids closed beneath
                              their sunny sheet…

The lips stammer against the light.
Sleep holds them, forming the oracle, saying:
'Able to touch'. I woke up, saying,
'I was able to touch his sorrow.'

Vernon had never before seen Dylan drunk; Wyn Lewis had never seen him drunk either, and Vernon did not tell him about the October celebration. It was, therefore, with confidence that, at the suggestion of Ian Watt, the Secretary of the Literary Society, he invited Dylan to Cambridge to give a talk. Since the publication of *Twenty-Five Poems* the new young poet had been a good deal talked about, and the Literary Society felt it quite a coup to have a member who had played croquet with him.

Dylan responded amiably but more practically than Wyn had expected; he asked for £5 and his expenses. This was a fairly large amount for an undergraduate Society in the thirties, but it was agreed on. The talk was to be a demolition of such contemporary giants as T. S. Eliot, Pound, Auden and Spender.

Neither of Dylan's biographers gives any account of this visit to Cambridge. Constantine FitzGibbon quotes a letter of February 11, from Dylan to David Higham, saying that he will be going to Cambridge the next day. Paul Ferris refers to a letter in the *T L S* in 1962, from Professor E. M. W. Tillyard, describing Dylan's 'feeble, maudlin state of intoxication' in an undergraduate's rooms. But Wyn Lewis gave me a very detailed account, which may perhaps show how much Dylan needed alcohol to face public occasions.

Wyn met Dylan at the railway station in mid-afternoon, and took him to his lodgings in Park Parade, where Ian Watt and tea were waiting. But Dylan told Wyn that he had already drunk thirty pints of beer and wanted more. (These thirty pints are almost certainly as illusory as the eighteen straight whiskies alleged to have been drunk in New York before Dylan's collapse.) Wyn would have been more apprehensive than he was if Dylan had not been so pleasantly mellow, talking of his own poetry and pleased that Wyn knew *Twenty-Five Poems* (a copy of which had, in fact, been pressed on him by Vernon soon after its publication.) He played with Wyn's piano, ate and drank tea, talked pleasantly to Patric Dickinson and other undergraduates, who came in after tea, and expanded pleasurably in their obvious admiration. Wyn and Ian felt that everything was going smoothly. It would probably have continued to go smoothly if they could have stayed in Park Parade until the talk began.

But they had been invited to a sort of cocktail party reception given by a wealthy South African undergraduate, and Dylan had to be half coaxed, half forced to go. He was always terrified of formal occasions, or occasions that he thought might be formal. His terror, as so often, showed as surliness and obstinacy. At last, Wyn and Ian Watt, both very tall, took Dylan's small, protesting body between them and bore him off.

A hush fell as they entered the host's plush rooms. He hurried over to them, carrying a tray of glasses full of South African sherry. His gushing welcome focussed attention on the newcomers, and Dylan almost had to be prevented from backing out of the door. Embarrassed and apprehensive, he downed a glass of sherry, which he hated, in one gulp, and, in the ensuing silence gulped another three in quick succession, crying, "More!" between each.

The sherry had an immediate effect. He aggressively demanded whisky, and while this was being fetched, his nonplussed host introduced him, by way of distraction, to the belle of the English faculty, a stunning young lady with (unfortunately, as it turned out) a double row of buttons placed at strategic intervals on her fine figure. At once, Dylan went into his Harpo Marx routine, which would have caused screams of laughter in his favourite London pubs – eyes bulging, twitching fingers outstretched, ready to pounce. But the young lady shrank back, dismayed, towards the protective frown of a don's wife. Nobody laughed. Dylan drowned his embarrassment in his whisky glass.

The disconcerted Secretary decided that his guest must be taken away. Wyn nervously said that poets had always been a law unto themselves, but an icy silence from the dons and their wives answered him. Dylan himself was unaffected. As he was borne away between his two guards, he shouted cheerfully back over his shoulder, "Goodbye, everybody, see you later." Then he wrenched himself free and rolled down the stairs.

Picked up and dusted, he was half-led, half-carried along Trinity Street, making obscene gestures and mouthing invitations to every passing woman. In the merciful dusk, he was at last led into Ian Watt's rooms in Ram Yard, where he stumbled to a couch and fell fast asleep. Ian and Wyn picked at the delicate crab salad and sipped white wine while Dylan snored.

At ten to eight, they could wait no longer. A bowl of water and a sponge, liberally applied, resulted in Dylan's sudden waking in a furious temper. He did not know where he was and, when told, refused to admit that he had ever agreed to address any sort of society. He staggered to a full-length Victorian mirror and addressed himself in scathing terms: "What do you think you're doing? Who *are* you, anyway? You tell the world who you are," while the waiting taxi ticked up the minutes.

At last, the two undergraduates became desperate, and almost manhandled their captive poet into the taxi. He was bitterly offended, but once in the taxi, he began to comb his hair, straighten his tie and feel for his notes. (The dinner-jacket borrowed for this occasion from Tom Warner was doubtless lying forgotten in his suitcase.) Wyn urged the taxi on, spurred by the thought of all those people who had been so indignant at the sherry party, growing even more indignant as they waited. It was already fifteen minutes later than the advertised time of the talk. When they arrived at St. John's, they hurried Dylan along the corridors, Wyn mentally composing some sort of apology. But, in the lecture-room, there was almost no-one to whom to apologise. Six students sat among a wilderness of chairs.

One of them told Wyn, in whispers, that all the dons and their wives had decided to boycott the talk and had advised the undergraduates to do the same. After a hasty consultation, Wyn and Ian left Dylan in charge of the audience, and rushed out, one into the college, the other into the street, where, like the servants at the Biblical wedding-feast, 'they gathered together all as many as they found, both bad and good.'

By half-past eight, with a couple of dozen more in the audience, Dylan asked peevishly, "Shall we begin now?" He slapped his thick script (about twenty pages covered with his miniscule handwriting) on the lectern, leaned over it and began muttering, but gradually a phrase or two, then a sentence, began to come clear, of such riveting quality that the audience sat up as though electrified. Gradually, the speaker got into his stride. For more than an hour he gave a pyrotechnic display of wild, brilliant, anarchic comments on the contemporary literary scene. Attracted by the shrieks of laughter, other people looked round the door and then sidled in. Long before the end of the talk, the room was crowded and people were standing in the corridor. When Dylan finally came to a stop, tremendous cheering and applause broke out, the audience crowded round him, and he was borne off to the rooms of Wyn's tutor, where he sat by the fire for hours, drinking coffee and telling Welsh stories to a fascinated and ever-growing crowd. It was a triumph snatched from the jaws of disaster, anticipating by twenty years similar evenings that were to take place in colleges all over America. Both Wyn and Dylan were euphoric as they trailed away to bed in the small hours of the morning, though Dylan was depressed at being left alone in the grand and rather sombre guest-room.

He was due to return to London the next morning. Wyn arrived at about nine o'clock to take him to the station. A gyp had brought him breakfast, but he was still in bed, bleary, sullen and coughing appallingly.

"Did they bring you a good breakfast?" Wyn asked politely.

Dylan's tone was intensely bitter. "Oh, yes, if you call about a pint of blood in your porridge *nice*," and after another frightful explosion of coughing, he held out a blood-stained handkerchief. Wyn was horrified. Was Dylan having a haemorrhage, like Keats? Would he die in the guest-room? Ought he to have a doctor, or be rushed to hospital? Dylan grumblingly got up and dressed, but refused to be taken to the station, on the grounds that he had accepted an invitation to lunch – where, he did not say. He disappeared shortly after, and Wyn lost track of him completely.

Occasionally, during the following week, they ran into each other, in the streets, in Sydney Sussex, in King's, in Magdalene. Dylan was enjoying himself tremendously, feted, lionised, and floating from college to college on a wave of adulation. His suitcase remained unopened in Wyn's rooms. One day it was not there.

Dylan did not always need drink – or, at least, not alcohol. He always needed a glass of something to sip, but he was satisfied with fizzy pop, with home-made lemonade, even, sometimes, at Heatherslade, with a glass of water. I have seen him spend a whole evening with Vernon and Fred Janes, reading and discussing the first draft of his *August Bank Holiday* script, with nothing but a single bottle of beer. When he was at ease, relaxed, and drinking only beer, nothing went wrong, but if he was under pressure or anxious and began to drink spirits, then trouble began.

Chapter 5

THE END OF AN ERA

There still lives the memory of those bygone years filled with warmth and laughter, a delicate sense of what was frail and yet unperishable in our adventure through life. – F. D-L.

In the autumn term of 1936, a young French *assistant* at the Swansea Grammar School was asked by D. J. Thomas to contribute a short article to the School magazine. Francis Dufau-Labeyrie was a Gascon from Dax, tall, dark, dark-eyed and apparently irresistible to ladies. He was a student at the Sorbonne, studying for the *agrégation* and complying with requirements by writing a thesis on Ernest Dowson. He gave conversation classes to the Grammar School boys, for which he received ten pounds a week.

His article was accepted by D. J. Thomas, who then suggested that he should meet Dylan, since they were both interested in English poetry. "My son…wants to become the Poet Laureate, or something like that."

One day early in 1937, Francis turned up at the Kardomah, and became for a short time, until Dylan left Swansea in April, his drinking companion. Dylan was at this time immensely attracted by the dockland area, where he and Francis would roam about in the dark, dropping in at small pubs and usually ending up at the Metropole Hotel, near the station, where a sumptuously-endowed young lady called Vera served. Francis recalled that one evening he had been invited to dinner at Cwmdonkin Drive. He and Dylan had a pre-dinner drink, which, unfortunately, went on till closing-time. Remorseful, nervous and quite drunk, they hurried, too late, up the hill, to be met by Mrs. Thomas's anxious rebukes. The elaborate dinner she had prepared was still being kept warm, although her husband had gone to bed in disgust. "Great was my embarrassment," wrote Francis, "and so was Dylan's. We apologised, and I remember how touching he was in his affectionate acceptance of his mother's scolding.

Francis had also become a great friend of Vernon's.

> Vernon soon invited me to meet his mother and father, with whom he lived in their lovely 'Heatherslade' home, on top of the Pennard cliffs. One Sunday morning in February or March, I set out by bus from Swansea. It snowed, and it snowed, and it snowed, as Dylan later wrote in *A Child's Christmas in Wales*, and the bus, a red double-decker affair transporting me as sole passenger, could not go beyond Bishopston. I got out there and trudged the rest of the long way, with the wind in my face, and ankle-deep in snow, to 'Heatherslade'…I clearly remember my hand on the latch, the click I still hear, distinctly, as I pushed the gate against the thick layer of snow behind it.

Vernon commemorated this first meeting in his poem *The Fire in the Snow*:

> Come in. The brilliant, beautiful
> Sun has dropped, and the noon-cracked pool
> Freezes back. Come, seek from night
> Gloom's fire, where the unlit room is white.
>
> I wait, intent, by the firelit stones
> Strewn with chopped wood and fallen cones.
> Come in, and watch with me in dark
> The red spark eating the black bark.
>
> Bright, from fields where the snow lies thick,
> From sunk fields to the latch's click
> You come, and your eyes, most watchful, glow
> Seeing in the darkness the brightness of snow.

Francis had lodgings at 11 Calvert Terrace, with a Mrs. James, an unusually tolerant landlady, who would pour out the tea for her lodger and his friends. She also allowed him to give small parties, at one of which Dylan attempted to shampoo the carpet with beer. Francis left

Swansea in July 1937, to spend the summer vacation in France, just before the momentous news of Dylan's marriage reached Vernon.

Dylan's letter with this announcement was characteristic of him; the news appeared only after an apology for altering one of Vernon's poems, and a discussion of the first number of *Wales*, a new magazine edited by Keidrych Rhys (who had been born Ronald Jones, and was unaware that there is no K in the Welsh language). Dylan had, ever since their first meeting, tried to persuade Vernon to publish some of his poems; he felt that there was an element of cowardice in an artist who refused to submit his work to public scrutiny. Keidrych had asked Dylan to look out for contributions for his first issue, and Dylan had picked up at Heatherslade two poems, *Griefs of the Sea* and *Old Triton Time*.

Vernon's pleasure at seeing his poems in print quickly changed to rage as he saw that *Griefs of the Sea* had been altered, and that the nature of the changes made it clear that Dylan was responsible.

> We had always agreed to suggest any improvement to each other in a poem where it seemed to go wrong, and in this particular poem Dylan had persuaded me to make one change of a word, but to alter a poem without the other's consent was to me unthinkable.

Furiously and in secret, Vernon spent all his lunch hours and the next Saturday afternoon after the publication of *Wales* making the necessary alteration in every copy of the magazine, in every bookshop in Swansea. He wrote Dylan a letter full of curses, beginning, "This is just to wish you an extra sweat in your worst nightmare."

Dylan apologised for the 'Thowdlerised' poem, giving an explanation for the changes which was almost certainly untrue. Only in the third paragraph of his letter did he tell Vernon about his marriage. It was not long before he brought Caitlin to the little house in Bishopston where his parents now lived. On 30th August, Vernon wrote to Francis about his first meeting with her.

Dylan came home with his wife Caitlin (Caitlin ni Houlihan)

last week and the first day he was home they came over here to supper. She is a beautiful and very nice girl, with wonderful gold hair like the incarnation of light, and still blue eyes like flowers. When she smokes a cigarette she looks very like Dylan, and her remarks are like his, but softer and in a lower key.

When their great friends marry, men are often distrustful or uneasy that their intimacy will wither away because of the new wife. If Vernon felt this at all, he never showed it. Caitlin simply became a part of the romantic aura in which Dylan lived in Vernon's mind. Passionate love merely completed the picture of Eurydice found, not lost, to live happy ever after in a world of pure poetry. Caitlin's beauty did indeed make her the perfect wife for a poet. In photographs she looks pretty, elegant, handsome, milk-maidish; but no photograph can show the loveliness of her colouring. Her hair really was 'wonderful'; in firelight or sunlight, it blazed with red-gold brilliance, her eyes were like cornflowers, and her complexion was as Yeats described Maud Gonne's, 'like light falling through the apple-blossom.' Before his death, Dylan is said to have spoken about his wife's radiance, of the 'illumination' about her. Certainly, I have seen her hair appear incandescent, as though it were actually shooting off sparkling rays into the ambient air when she shook her head. When Dylan and Vernon were watching her feeding Llewellyn, Dylan said, "What I love about Caitlin is that she changes all the time. One day she will look quite plain, then, she will be so beautiful that you can't look at her without being struck blind."

Vernon found her beauty remarkable, and commemorated it in several poems. 'That golden wife', he called her in one. She had entered the charmed circle in which Dylan lived, and was thereafter to be immune from criticism, as he was. However outrageous her behaviour was in later years, Vernon accepted it. Only once, when she was dissatisfied with a performance of *Figaro*, saying savagely, "Oh, if even Mozart lets you down...!" was he slightly deprecatory. He would never take sides with one or the other in their frequent quarrels, preferring to think that these were a mere facade, as indeed they sometimes were. One night when they had been quarrelling so violently in a pub that even Vernon began to feel anxious, they fell into each other's arms the moment they arrived at Sea View, giggling and congratulating each other on the tremendous show they had put on for the regulars.

But the real quarrels came later. Wyn Lewis remembers Caitlin, in the first months of the marriage, as being quiet, almost withdrawn, enigmatically silent among the chatterers, totally absorbed by Dylan, attentive to every word and gesture of his, seeming to be completely devoted to him. A photograph of her at this time expresses this very well; as oblivious of the camera as of the hole in her jersey, she rests her head against Dylan's breast, a look of dreamy happiness on her beautiful face,

Her devotion to and absorption in Dylan were so like Vernon's own that he felt no jealousy of the marriage. It has been suggested by both FitzGibbon ("ethereal… other-worldly… his gossamer-like personality…") and Ferris ("…gentle, even-tempered") that Vernon was constitutionally sweet-natured and that it was therefore easy for him to tolerate Dylan's vagaries and weaknesses. But this was not his nature at all. His standards for his family and friends were exacting, and he could be harsh if they were not adhered to; without being at all judgemental, he did demand that certain guide-lines for conduct be observed. He was never in the least afraid to speak his mind, to colleagues in the Air Force or the Bank, even to an Air Commodore who had not treated his recently published book of poems seriously. (This is why he did not get a commission!)

He could be infinitely patient over poetry, waiting years for a line to work itself out, but in all other ways he was extremely impatient. He would always prefer to walk rather than wait a few moments for a bus. On one occasion he bodily up-ended a grandfather clock that would not go, and on another he battered into a sheet of metal an oil-stove whose wick he could not turn down. Verbally too he could be unexpectedly aggressive; a mere corporal himself, he told the senior NCOs of the RAF Police that he never expected to meet at any other station in Britain

Francis Dufau-Labeyrie at Heatherslade, Winter 1937

"a bigger bunch of crooks". His manner could be, and often was, vague and dreamily courteous, what my father called 'half-soaked', and a Bletchley friend referred to as 'safe in the arms of Jesus.' But when really angered, he could project (without being violent) a devastating harshness. So, if Dylan could get away with anything, where Vernon was concerned, it was not at all because Vernon was a soft touch: if he could do no wrong in Vernon's eyes, it was because he was unique. He might alter poems, he might not turn up for a wedding, but Vernon had, once and for all, perceived the immense burden of genius under which he lived, and could tolerate any shortcomings in his daily life.

After their visit to Bishopston, when they saw Vernon several times, and Caitlin was initiated into croquet, Dylan and Caitlin stayed with Caitlin's mother in Hampshire until the spring of 1938. In February, Dylan sent Vernon a photograph of himself:

> It's one of many: this is the toughest. Why I want you to think of me – photographically, when I'm not about – as a tough, I don't know. Anyway, it's very big: you can write a poem on the back, draw whiskers on it, or advertize Kensitas in the front window.

The photograph, carelessly stuck in a thin envelope, arrived with several creases and a crack down its length. Dylan did look tough, like a handsome young gangster lighting a last cigarette in a doorway before moving in for the kill. And Vernon did write a poem (though not on its back) in which he tried to resolve some of the contradictions which he felt to be inherent not only in Dylan's nature but in their friendship. He called it *Portrait of a Friend*.

> He has sent me this
> Late and early page
> Caught in the emphasis
> Of last night's cartonnage,
> Crumpled in the post,
> Bringing to lamplight
> Breath's abatement
> Mute as a mummy's pamphlet
> Long cherished by a ghost.
>
> Trusting a creaking house
> His roof is ruinous,
> So mortal. A real wind
> Beats on this house of sand
> Two tides like ages buffet.
> The superhuman, crowned
> Saints must enter this drowned
> Tide-race of the mind
> To guess or understand
> The face of this cracked prophet,

Which from its patient pall
I slowly take,
Drop the envelope,
Compel his disturbing shape,
And write these words on a wall
Maybe for a third man's sake.

(Dylan is said by Constantine FitzGibbon to have read this poem aloud in the spring of 1944, and, on closing the book, to have remarked, 'in an entirely matter-of-fact tone of voice', to his future biographer, "And of course the third man, Constantine, is you.")

While Dylan was in Hampshire, he kept up a fairly regular correspondence with Vernon. Each sent poems of his own and criticised the other's poems. Dylan called his long poems 'exhausters'; Vernon preferred to call a long poem an 'opus', which naturally made the short ones into opossums. Dylan sent 'my sixty-line year's work', which turned out to be the poem to Caitlin, *I Make This in a Warring Absence,* and 'one I have spent a great deal of time on', which was the first part of *In Memory of Ann Jones*, both afterwards to become anthology pieces. Vernon was to write afterwards of his excitement when he first saw these poems.

Still, he was glad when Dylan came back to Bishopston in early April 1938. In his edition of the letters, he says that Dylan spent three months staying with his parents; it was in fact less than two, since, on the 9th May, Vernon wrote to Francis describing his first visit to their new home in Gosport Street, saying that, before they went away, he had been seeing a great deal of them 'every other day.'

Caitlin especially would have been glad to get away from Bishopston to Heatherslade, where she could sunbathe, walk on the cliffs, run down to any of the bays within half-a-mile of the house to swim – always her great passion, and, in the evenings, listen silently to Dylan and Vernon reading poetry, play croquet, or sometimes, *Lexicon,* that pleasant forerunner of *Scrabble,* at which she was always beaten by the others. But once, when Vernon's mother was playing too, Caitlin's face lit up, and she prepared to lay down a word. Dylan, curious, looked over her shoulder, and immediately put his hand over her cards. "No, Cat, no," he said, his face a mixture of amusement and consternation, "no, really, you can't put that down."

"Can't put it down!" she said, bewildered. "But K is six, and ING gets a lot too!" She assumed that this was a plot on Dylan's part to prevent her winning; but nothing can show more clearly the chasm between her background and Dylan's.

The young couple must have been given something to start housekeeping with in the first Gosport Street weeks, for Vernon wrote to Francis, "I brought small provisions like tinned fruit from Carmarthen market, but they already had a lot." Soon, however, the usual shortage of money set in, and for a short time they gave up cigarettes. "He and Caitlin both smoke a pipe," wrote Vernon, "often sharing one." On the 16th June, Dylan wrote to Henry Treece, "I haven't a single penny, a half-penny, or filed French slot-coin… Bitter, cruel, Laugharne, my pipe is full of butt-ends from the grate."

It was Richard Hughes, author of the best-seller *A High Wind in Jamaica,* who had found the little house in Gosport Street for them. Dylan wrote rather misleadingly to Treece, "The village also contains bearded Richard High-Wind Hughes, but we move, in five hundred yards, in two or more different worlds: he owns the local castle, no roof and all, and lives in a grand mansion by its side and has a palace in Morocco." This implied that the two worlds were separate, whereas Hughes regularly invited the couple to lunch or dinner, gave them money, and, in 1941, invited them to stay at the Castle while he served in the Navy. Vernon met him for the first time on his May visit to Laugharne. He described the meeting in a letter to Francis:

> … in walked Richard Hughes like a very rich, bearded telegraph post. Electric messages of an avuncular kind trickled from his beard as he stood quite still, never looking at me but straight ahead of him as if a spider were hanging halfway between him and the person he was talking to. He was nice but I was glad when he went… Dylan says his wife is so rich she can't hold her eyelids up…

February 1938. "You can… write a poem on the back…"

Vernon was later to enlarge his account of this interview for his foreword to *A High Wind in Jamaica*.

The sun now lit up the newly-painted room where we had breakfast, and we had just finished when there were two knocks on the door. "That will be Hughes," said Dylan. This visitation gave the surname an accent of awe.

If the awe of expectation was considerable, the awe of the presence was much greater. I saw in the doorway a figure tall and solemn, with a high, white forehead and black, curly beard, his powerful hands resting on a strong cane. On this he leaned in order not to dwarf still further the low doorway on whose threshold he stood. I was quickly introduced, and he moved with an evenness of step and intonation into the room, rising there almost to the raftered ceiling, and then standing stock-still opposite the window, black-bearded and impressive, like a sea-captain who had taken up a vantage-point in a small boat, focussing, with an invisible telescope, on something none of us could see. His eye travelled from the white rafters round the walls of the room to the floor, and ours followed his until all our heads were inclined down. "I like your lilac-coloured beams," he said. Our eyes shot up incredulously to the beams that had seemed white, while he, too, studied them. He murmured without changing his posture, "And I like the feet of your table."

In June, Vernon and Francis went to Ireland, to visit W. B. Yeats. That visit, long looked forward to, is commemorated in Vernon's long poem *Yeats in Dublin*. On the way back, cycling from Fishguard to Laugharne 'on saddles that bruised us unmercifully'; they spent two days with Dylan and Caitlin.

When I stayed with Dylan Thomas in Laugharne on my way back from seeing Yeats in Dublin in the summer of 1938, I was struck by the difference between them. Both were men of undoubted genius, but whereas Yeats spoke like a musically controlled oracle, Dylan Thomas, with his abundant imagination and quick intelligence was prepared to challenge everything he said. Not that Dylan Thomas did not admire Yeats's poetry immensely, because he did. But he distrusted, at the age of twenty-three, pontifical statements, or statements that sounded pontifical. Yeats had told me, "There must always be a quality of nonchalance in a poet's work." Dylan would not accept this. And Yeats had added, "The young poets toil too much."

"He should come *here*," Dylan said.

In July, Dylan and Caitlin moved from Gosport Street to a larger house, Sea View. The weekend before they moved was spent in Bishopston, almost certainly to beg, borrow or steal some household equipment for their new six-roomed mansion. On the Saturday night, Vernon's mother took them all to the theatre, to see a Noel Coward play. Vernon reported to Francis that Dylan said he was sorry they had to rush back to Laugharne so quickly, that after 'sweet aloes', they had left with 'bitter goodbyes'

Vernon admired the huge, new, four-storey house, "which is like a house in a fairy tale, and is one. The basement," he told Francis, "has hooks on the ceiling and we hung on one of them a slab of meat which I'd bought for them in Carmarthen market. You would make short work of it but it would last them, perhaps, 4 days. We couldn't hang the cheese."

Early in September, a memorable visit took place, which Dylan still remembered two years later.

"I didn't tell you," Vernon wrote to Francis, "that we all went down there to see them in Wyn Lewis's car. Wyn wasn't there, but David Lewis drove… We all went down to Pendine sands where everyone in turn… drove the car. I was the only one who, after at least twenty attempts, failed to start it. Even Dylan succeeded, and with the throttle full out managed to do 10 miles an hour – in soft sand. Then everyone had to get out and heave the car out of it. Caitlin drove well, so did David's friend, and I grew very jealous and pleaded for one more try. I had it, and when I sailed past Dot and Fig at 50 miles an hour, Fig's only comment to Dot was, 'This is the end.'"

In the autumn of 1938, Dylan read two short poems on the BBC. Vernon and his sister, in full evening dress, went to a concert in the Brangwyn Hall; after the concert, they took a bus to the house of Francis's former landlady, 'broke in on her and without overture or explanation switched on the wireless – Why? – For Dylan's broadcast – Missed the last bus – got home by taxi.'

Francis was now an assistant teacher at the Beckenham and Penge County School for Boys. His landlady was very different from the Swansea one; she had platinum hair and a shapely figure. Francis told Vernon that one of his friends, calling to see him and being told, "Mr Labeyrie isn't here; he comes and goes, you know," had said, with an admiring look, "I expect he comes more often than he goes." He had in common with Vernon and Dylan a passionate interest in words, and his grasp of the nuances of colloquial English is impressive.

"Your idea of going to Chatham (for conversation) is very acceptable," he wrote, "but why not take a few books with us and meet at Reading? Or shall I wheel you in a pram up to Motherwell? Or else we could absorb a comfortable quantity of Bile Beans and suddenly wake up for a meeting in Liverpool?" He was fascinated by Dylan's work, and in 1937 had completed his first translation of the short story *A Prospect of the Sea,* which he had read in the Spring issue of *Life and Letters Today.* Vernon helped with explanations and suggestions, and the first version was shown to Dylan. Though his knowledge of French was rudimentary, he listened with interest and helped to ensure that the translation was as accurate as possible in the rendering of fine shades of meaning. Jose Corti, a well-known Parisian publisher of the time, who had made a name by promoting the then avant-garde French writers, including the surrealists, was very much interested in *Perspective Sur la Mer*. But Dylan was then completely unknown in France so it could not be published in 'plaquette' form without some preliminary funding. In the event, it was published in the 1946 issue of *L'Arche*, an advanced literary review edited by Jean Anvrouche and Dominique Aury. Francis also translated *The Orchards* and *The Map of Love,* and, after the war, was to translate the whole of *Portrait of the Artist as a Young Dog*. 1938 was the year of Munich, and it became obvious that war was inevitable, sooner or later. But Vernon thought Dylan was happier at Sea View than he ever would be again. The inevitable money worries seemed not to be of great importance, and, in any case, Vernon could always, on his visits, produce pleasure with gifts of banknotes, food or books. Any quarrels were still lovers' quarrels. Vernon once offered to help clear the table after a meal, but Dylan said, "No, the woman does all that. We must get on with our poems." Caitlin was not always so complaisant, though. On one visit, Vernon took a bag of ripe plums, and Dylan, stretched out on the sofa, asked for one. Caitlin snatched the bag from under Vernon's outstretched hand and snapped, "No; he has to get up and fetch a plum if he wants one." There was a silence, broken by a soft wheedling voice from the sofa. "Ca-at. Can I have a plum?" Absolute silence. "Ca-at. Can I have a plum; just one?" Silence. "Ca-at?"

Still in fierce silence, Caitlin turned on her way out to the kitchen and bombarded him savagely with every plum in the bag. He lay quite still with his eyes closed until the rain of fruit had stopped, then, thoughtfully sucking a plum which had fallen on his lap, he said, "Right. Now shall we get on with our poems?"

The poems they were getting on with that summer and autumn were revisions of *Portrait of a Friend, The Collier, Call It All Names* and a translation of Novalis's hymn *Wenn Alle Untreu Werden*. "That hymn must be great in the original," wrote Dylan. "I wish I could read German." Vernon also introduced Dylan to Spanish poetry that summer. "I went over to Bishopston," he wrote to Francis in September, "taking with me Lorca and a book of Welsh translations from Taliesin... We read a lot of Lorca which is grand – I found I knew about half of it by heart." He also helped Dylan write a short appreciation of T. S. Eliot for the Harvard University magazine, as he had helped him with his contribution to the Auden double number of *New Verse*. ("Congratulations on Auden's seventieth birthday," was its characteristic conclusion.)

The poems Dylan had written during this time were *On No Work of Words Now, The Tombstone Told When She Died, A Saint About To Fall,* and the *Birthday Poem.* (Twenty-four years remind the tears of my eyes.) "I cannot describe my excitement when I saw (it) for the first time on a postcard," Vernon wrote in his edition of Dylan's letters. He had suggested that *A Saint About to Fall* should be called *Poem In the Ninth Month,* and this title was used at the poem's first printing in *Poetry (London).* When it appeared in *The Map of Love,* and later in *Collected Poems,* the first line was used as title.

Dylan was at this time working on the stories which were later to be collected in *Portrait of the Artist.* These stories represented a real change in both style and attitude, a change observed by the only critic who at that time was following Dylan's work as closely as Dylan himself. He wrote:

> In the prose, too, there came recurrent moments of severe self-appraisal, when what had seemed to be a masterpiece at the time of writing appeared to be in retrospect only a *tour de force.* The highly-charged language of the symbolic stories reached its climax in what was to be his most ambitious story, the opening of which he left as a fragment called *In the Direction of the Beginning.* He told me after this that he would never again write a story of that kind, and at the same time his verse underwent a profound change, not exactly of language, but of approach. The change was, I think, heralded by the little poem which begins:
>
> > Once it was the colour of saying...
>
> This, and the other poems of *The Map of Love,* showed that, while he had now resolved to write only stories about real

people, his poetry had also moved in the direction of the living voice.

If it was the end of an era in Dylan's work, it was also the end of an era in his life. "You know I'm going to be a father in January," he wrote. And the war was coming nearer. But however dramatic the new life, however brilliant the new work, the old life and the old work had been good. It was the Laugharne days that Vernon commemorated in his poem *To A Shell*:

> At last, beautiful shell,
> Lie there crushed: but the sea
> Cannot obliterate yet
> Faith I remember well:
> A house facing the sea.
> Hard and bitterly
> Though waves beat on that wall
> From the swirling quicksands of debt,
> I swear that it cannot fall.
>
> Nor can you drag those words,
> Confident in their day,
> Down to the unknown deep.
> I have a net whose cords
> Gather the fallen day
> And make the forgotten stay
> In all but the detail death
> Moves to the realm of sleep,
> So strong is the pledge of breath.
>
> And though the magical dice
> Loaded for nothing, toss
> All to perdition, left
> In darkness, held in a vice
> No white breaker can toss
> All to a total loss.
> Still the relic will hold,
> Caught in a secret cleft,
> Tenderer light than gold.

All I remember, all
Of the locked, unfolding days
Where tomorrow's treasure shines.
Fragile nautilus caul,
Tell the fingers of days:
'Find me. Enter the praise
Of Eden's morning, inlaid
With dazzling, intimate lines.
Touch, and the world will fade.'

Dylan and Caitlin at Heatherslade, August 1937

Chapter 6

THE EDGE OF THE ABYSS

He told me that he was writing a new poem… It was to be called 'Deaths and Entrances' because, he said, it was all he had ever written about or wanted to write about. – V. W.

The year 1939 began with death and birth. On the 28th January Yeats died; on the 30th Dylan's son was born.

Vernon was devastated by the news of Yeats's death. He wrote at once to Francis:

"I expect you were awake last night too. What is to be said? Yeats himself has said the last word:

'Now that my ladder's gone,
I must lie down where all the ladders start
In the foul rag-and-bone shop of the heart.'

"… Yesterday, before hearing the news, I had talked to my father a lot about Yeats's illness, about his going to Menton for the winter. I had no actual premonition of immediate death, yet the news of his death came as no surprise. I was in this room… and mother shouted through the partition. I said 'I know' quite evenly. When you rang up I was still in a pretty incoherent state!"

He later wrote of this moment in *The Mummy*:

What shudder of birth or death? What shakes me most?
Job his Maker answering, the Stricken exclaiming 'Rejoice!'
Gripping late in the shifting moment giant Earth,
making Earth a ghost
Who heard a great friend's death without a change of voice.

Dylan and Caitlin were in Hampshire. When their baby was two days old, Dylan wrote to Vernon, "I'm sorry Yeats is dead. What a loss of the great poems he would write. Aged 73, he died in his prime." He, too, looked back over the year that was gone, in a small poem sent to Vernon in February, with the provisional title of *January 1939*. This was the famous poem that begins:

> Because the pleasure-bird whistles after the hot wires,
> Shall the blind horse sing sweeter?

over which James Agate was so gleeful, in his column in the *Daily Express*. The image of the singing horse came from a dream of Dylan's, in which a horse stood in a cage of wires that gradually became red-hot, on which a man standing by said, "He sings better now."

But I wonder if the poem was not also unconsciously influenced by Hardy's *The Blinded Bird*:

> So zestfully canst thou sing?
> And all this indignity,
> With God's consent, on thee!
> Blinded ere yet a-wing
> By the red-hot needle thou,
> I stand and wonder how
> So zestfully thou canst sing!

Dylan's poem shows the poet 'an enamoured man alone with the twigs of his eyes'…. 'turning to stare at an old year'. And although he says, "This present grace over the past table," the future seems to be at best enigmatic and at worst sinister. Indeed, Dylan wrote to Bert Trick in March 1939, "We're all moving away. And every single decisive action happens in a blaze of disappointment." If Dylan, twenty-four years old, not two years married, and the father of a six-month-old son, really felt this disappointment, then the years that were gone must have meant more to him than those to come. Constantine FitzGibbon comments:

> Dylan's nostalgia for the past, for that lost paradise of innocence which we all carry with us throughout lives that are seldom innocent and never paradisiac, became henceforth an ever stronger theme in his writing… And in his later poems, which

he once defined to a journalist as 'statements on the way to the grave', this emotion is of far greater complexity, and nostalgia itself becomes an inadequate word with which to define it.

Still, for the time being, he was coming back to Laugharne, and Vernon waited impatiently for his return. He wrote to Francis in March:

Dylan will be in Bishopston at Easter for a day with Caitlin and his boy... He's bringing out a book of poems and 7 stories with a portrait by John, to cost 7/6. *A Prospect of the Sea* was refused on the grounds of its 'unwarrantable moments of sensuality'. Can you beat that? It's like telling somebody to write with his hands in a muff... It convinces me that publishers' heads are full of sawdust, that their eyes are really buttons.

Vernon had no time for editors, publishers, critics or just plain readers who did not appreciate Dylan's work. Long after Dylan's death, he wrote about the two 'birth poems' at the end of *The Map of Love*

The second of these two poems was to be a dialogue between an unborn child and its mother, and it was about this that Robert Graves, who has so many children but doesn't seem to know how they are born, showed such ignorance and obtuseness in his Clark lecture.

Dylan's work was sacrosanct, but even his actions were not to be lightly criticised. Because he had not heard a broadcast of Dylan's, Francis was called, 'You wart, blain, pimple, boil, pig's trotter, skunk's tail, swollen toe, female flea...'; but when Dylan failed to turn up in Swansea for the performance of Vernon's masque, *The Influences*, Vernon made many, often incompatible excuses. Two performances were given by the Swansea Little Theatre, on the 6th and 7th July. On the 4th Dylan wrote:

This is to tell you, with great regret, that we *may* not be able to come to your play. If Hughes can come... then we'll be able to; if not, not. I thought I'd some money this week, but bills took it at once and now we couldn't afford to go to Carmarthen even.

On the 6th, Vernon had a telegraph from Dylan to say that he was coming; but in the event, although Richard and Frances Hughes turned up, Dylan did not. A letter to Francis on the 7th says, "Last night was momentous. The masque was glorious... How I wish you could have been there! Nearly everyone was, except Dylan and Caitlin who were kept away by horrible colds." However horrible his cold, it did not prevent Dylan from visiting Bishopston almost immediately after the second performance, for the two weeks that Vernon was away on his annual vacation. Yet, in a broadcast interview with Robin Holmes in 1957, when Holmes said, "In your book (of Letters) he does treat you rather carelessly on occasion, apparently – he didn't for instance come to the Masque," Vernon was quick to defend Dylan, by saying, "Well, that was a question of money with the Masque; unfortunately, he ran out of funds, he would certainly have come..."

But, in the spring of 1939, all that was in the future: Dylan was back in Wales. On April 15th, Vernon wrote to Francis:

> I'm incredibly happy too... Yes, and you must congratulate me as well, because I'm now a father. Don't be alarmed. Dylan made me godfather to his child, and he was proxy for me. He rushed into the house last Saturday and asked me to come to the christening but I had to perform my blessing by proxy. I got the christening present for Llewellyn yesterday – a silver spoon and fork, – very lovely. I'll go to Laugharne next weekend, I expect.

Early in January, Vernon bought the married couple another present. Dylan had long wanted a radio, and Vernon bought him one. All three were as unmechanical as possible, and Dylan wrote:

> Is the wireless, please, A. C. or D. C.? The expert here can't tell and daren't test it until he knows for certain; he might blow it up... It's still in Billy Williams's – he's the local electrician. He wanted me to get hold of the set's book of instructions for

him, or, at any rate a little 3 plug lead which is supposed to go
in at the back of the machine but which wasn't among the parts
you gave me.

Such was the expertise of Laugharne's electrician that the set was still
not installed by the middle of May. But Vernon did not mind. He wrote
to Francis on 21st May:

> I spent last weekend with Dylan at Laugharne. He's much
> bigger all round – 12 stone 8 – but otherwise very much the
> same. We had a long confab. with Richard Hughes in which
> I took no part. And I cycled home in the dark without a lamp
> of any kind.

The baby Llewellyn was a new element in the visits. Although Vernon
was over thirty, he had no young married friends or relatives, and therefore
no acquaintance with babies or small children. Bachelors are usually either
cynical or romantic about marriage; Vernon was romantic. Caitlin had
been aureoled with Dylan's glory, now their son shone in his rays. Caitlin
suckling her baby became almost a Madonna in Vernon's eyes, and,
indeed, he named a sonnet written at this time *The Mother and Child*.

> Let hands be about him white, O his mother's first,
> Who caught him, fallen from light through nine months' haste
> Of darkness, hid in the worshipping womb, the chaste
> Thought of the creature with its certain thirst.
> Looking up to her eyes declined that made her fair
> He kicks and strikes for joy, reaching for those dumb springs.
> He climbs her, sinks and his mouth under darkness clings
> To the night-surrounded milk in the fire of her hair.
>
> She drops her arm, and, feeling the fruit of his lips,
> Tends him cunningly. O what secrets are set
> In the tomb of each breath, where a world of light in eclipse
> Of a darkly worshipping world exults in the joy she gave
> Knowing that miracle, miracle to beget,
> Springs like a star to her milk, is not for the grave.

Vernon's attitude to Llewellyn was one of wary reverence: he took his duties as godfather very seriously. He sent money when he could, always remembered Christmas and birthday presents, and when he wrote poems for or about Dylan or Llewellyn, faithfully remitted the payments to Laugharne. The first poem for his godson was to accompany the christening spoon:

> There in the velvet lies
> Near your blue eyes,
> Enclosed in its own silences
> A spoon...
>
> It mirrors back a wave,
> Silver and grave,
> From expectation's haunted cave,
> In which your bigger eyes one day may see
> A tall house leaning, open to the sea.
>
> And there the sudden tide
> Flooding the wide
> Mud-hollows at the Castle's side,
> Pounds tongues with light, and, breaking language down,
> Brings to our ears the Portreeve's fishing-town.

Of eight short poems for Llewellyn, which appeared in the August 1940 issue of *Life and Letters Today*, the third describes the threat always hanging about the little family:

> Fingers of poverty faintly knock.
> Here, where is written in breath
> Blake's immortality sleeping in the rock,
> For a father who trusts in death.

The fourth poem holds a reference to one of Dylan's own letters, in which he had written, "... the ravens − soft, white, silly ravens − will feed us."

> Softer than all things but
> The youngest leaves,
> Cheek in love's shade lies safe: your eyes are shut
> Beneath the faint lids nobody believes
> Can hide the sailing heavens
> But he who stands

> By unicorn and tree beneath the ravens
> Whose claws have dropped their bread into his hands.

The sixth poem, six lines long, paints a tiny domestic scene in Sea View:

> Birds I remember, solitary birds,
> While I was looking, osiers wreathing
> Your cradle hung. That golden wife
> Stooped, and left in the room three words,
> Alone here breathing:
> 'A little life.'

These poems were written for Llewellyn's first birthday; for his second, Vernon wrote one called *Llewellyn's Chariot* (though it did not appear in the magazine until March 1943). This poem originated in an episode when Vernon slept in the same room as the baby, then aged about eighteen months. The cot was on the other side of the room from the visitor's bed; but at dawn Vernon woke to find the cot, driven on its castors by the child's strong agitations of its bars, bumping up against the bed, with Llewellyn staring at him from enormous blue eyes. Vernon saw the voyage as another Argosy, and the child's gold hair as the golden fleece. The poem ends:

> And I, your listener, stopped on the stairway of breath,
> Awake, in the stranger's bed, in the cold, high room,
> Calling the sea from Leviathan hollows of earth,
> I watch them, castaway toys, while you drive and boom
> Your course in the cot to my bed, with the speed of ice,
> The giant mirror, the trumpet ringed with a bell,
> Till naked you stand, gold-fleeced, shaping, a shell,
> All seas to your colour, Llewellyn, child above price.

It was to this poem that Dylan referred, five years later, in the Boar's Head in Carmarthen. We had been having lunch as Llewellyn charged and banged against tables, unreproved by either parent as he sang and shouted, until at last we were asked to leave. As we trailed out in disgrace, Dylan murmured apologetically, "Llewellyn, child below mice!"

Vernon usually wrote a birthday poem for his godson. *A Child's Birthday* was published in *Horizon* when Llewellyn was three (and later in *The Lady with the Unicorn*). An ingenious poem, *To My Godson*, was a kind of acrostic, in which the initial letters of each word, whether read forwards or backwards, read LLEWELLYN THOMAS:

> Life's leaven: eleven. Wake early, Llewellyn.
> You nearly touch heaven. O morning and song!
> Silence and music of happiness telling
> Name you Love's Easter: Wake early. Live long.

In spite of the darkening shadow of war, the summer of 1939 was a happy one for Vernon. He went to Laugharne as often as he could, not only to read and talk about poetry, but to walk on the sands, to drink in the pub, to sit in the sunny living-room in the evening while Llewellyn was being bathed, fed and put to bed; to listen to Dylan reading many of the stories for *Portrait of the Artist as a Young Dog*.

> The stories released a stream of humorous invention which Dylan had kept out of his poetry but which was very much a part of himself... My only objection to the *Portrait of the Artist* stories was the title. I thought the book ought to be called *One Warm Saturday*, after the last story. But Dylan was firm. Besides, his publishers had said that it was a good selling title. I could not see how the stories, as reproductions of his boyhood, could be improved, but he used to say that although he was very glad he had written them they could not compare with Joyce's *Dubliners*. Perhaps not. But I do not believe for a moment that Joyce could have written *The Peaches, The Fight,* or *Extraordinary Little Cough*.

Sometimes Vernon would read to Dylan, even Kierkegaard; but I think his own passion for that gloomy Dane misled him into thinking that the reading 'pierced Dylan deeply.' Yeats they both enjoyed and Dylan thought Rilke a great poet, but 'a very odd boy indeed.' But what Dylan liked very much were readings, or performances, from a Watkins family classic; this was the famous Italian Grammar, a Manual of Conversation English / Italian with the Italian figured pronunciation for English tourist in Italy. Most compilers of phrase-books prefer to remain anonymous, but our Professor BARONE lavishly displays his personality throughout his creation, which, by the way, is no mere phrase-book. He loved the English language second only to his own, and wished to show his extraordinary familiarity with its beauties and flexibility. Dylan and Vernon loved him, and regarded him as a fellow-creator.

The book opens with an announcement that the Italian *abbici* has five wowels and seventeen consonants. To show that this is no mere misprint, the chapter on WOWELS then begins, and the word is so spelt throughout the book (consistency is the Professor's strong point); as in 'if the verb ends in a wowel, the initial letter of the pronoun is doubled and the last wowel of the werb lose the accent.' Even in mere grammatical examples, his personal style reveals itself. Dylan was particularly fond of the negative imperatives, especially the imploring, 'Let them not chock with thirst,' and the anguished, 'Do not let him sing!' He also felt that as an example of the pluperfect, 'He had had a hat,' could hardly be bettered.

The chapter on Nomenclature fascinated him, especially the section on Parts of the Human Body, the end of which, he once said to Vernon, might be taken as a worksheet for one of his own early poems:

> The bones, the marrow, the nerves, an articulation,
> Humours, the blood, the bile, spittle
> Tears, sweat, milk, urine,
> The corpse.
> A skeleton.

He threatened, before his child's birth, to name it only from Barone's section on Proper Names, where he could choose from among such names as Bab, Balthasar, Hilairy, Hippolyt, Hug (sic) and Hyacinthus; Theobald, Tommy, Urban and Ulric. Vernon's sister suggested that if the baby proved to be twins, they should be called Ferocity and Insanity.

Having studied the vocabularies, the earnest student was invited to commit to memory certain 'preparatory phrases', designed to bring together what he had learned about grammar and words. Of these Dylan's favourite was the memorable sequence:

> Let me love my duty
> Let her love her grandsons
> Let us love our step-daughters

> Love you ancestors
> Let them love their family
> It is your duty to love your parents
> That loving child has ben sick!

But it is in the little conversational scenes, on various occasions and in various localities, that Barone's genius blazes most brightly. Not for him dull requests and duller replies, nor even the postilion struck by lightning – no, his characters are all aspiring Oscar Wildes, his ripostes sparkle. Even the paper-seller ("Sir, we have of the *Times*, the *Telegraph* and the *Tit-bits!*") has a certain flourish. The tramway conductor is formidable:

> Here is your ticket. Take care about not lose it. If a controller should arrive, he would let pay to you a double ticket. Conductor, will you let stop or no? I have sounded twice and the mechanician does not stop. *And it is just.* We have many stations for stopping for which one is not here.

The telephone operator, too, burns with a hard, gem-like flame:

> Miss, give me please, a communication.
> There's!
> Are you there?
> Why, which number do you vish?
> Give me please the 21065.
> Miss, they have taken away the communication!
> Certainly. Are already passed the five minutes.

Dylan and Vernon both agreed that Barone's masterpiece was the scene at the dentist's – a view shared, incidentally, by John Lennon in the sixties. He used the scene, transcribed verbatim, except for a few additions of his own, which greatly detracted from its impact, in his book, *In His Own Write*. Dylan liked to take the part of the dentist, with a strong Italian accent. Vernon was a sheepish and giggling patient; acting was never his strong point.

> I have a hollow tooth that makes me suffer dreadfully.
> Sit down in that armchair, madam, throw your head back and open your mouth wide. Ho! Your mouth is pretty clear of teeth!
> Alas! I have but eight left.
> Then you have lost twenty four.
> Impossible!

• • •

Let me see the tooth. Is it that one?
Yes sir! Could you not stop it up.
Stopping up teeth is only a palliative.
You will pull it out for me then?
No madam. I will extract it.
But that is very painful!
Not at all. It is a very easy operation, even not unaccompanied with a
certain pleasure... when it is over. Come, be courageous.
But! sir...
Let me only take out the cotton you have put in the hollow of the
tooth. Crack! there it is.
But sir, I was anxious to keep that tooth.
That was impossible. It is black and decayed. Besides, you have none
but old stumps in your mouth.

When Dylan went to what he called 'a very posh dentist', just before
he went to America, he sent Vernon a grinning miniature photograph
with the words, 'I have none but old stumps in my mouth,' scribbled
across it.

The finale of the Barone performance was always *Going To Bed*:

I confess that I am very tired. I am going to undress and get to bed
directly; in five minutes I shall be no more of this world. Have you
closed the shutters?
Yes sir, but perhaps you had better leave them open.
Why so?
To see the sun the sooner when you wak. (sic).
I declare myself unworthy to see the orb of day! All I know is that I
am ready to fall with sleep...O blissful bed! Blessed be the man who
invented beds.
That is your evening prayer?
My dear friend, you bore me considerably.
Let me sleep.

"My dear friend, you bore me considerably," was often used by Dylan
to defuse an argument over poetry when it became too heated. He could
reject criticism of his own poems very tolerantly; it was Vernon who
might flare up if Dylan suggested emendations.

Another favourite occupation was to revise or improve lines from well-known poems. 'Nobbly, nobbly, Cape St. Vincent,' was one; 'My name is Oswald J. Mandias, King of Kings' was another. 'It was a summer evening, old Kafka's work was done,' was a third. Then there were the original poems of which each poet had to compose an alternate line. One of these was an interminable ballad called *The Cosmopolitan Secret Agent*, which had new verses added at intervals. One verse will suffice to show its soporific quality:

> I'd like to lurk in the woods with a Turk,
> I'd like to sit on a Lapp;
> I'd like to lie with an Austrian spy,
> I'd like to Nippon a Jap.

Occasionally, they would compose pornographic couplets or quatrains, which Dylan one day suggested that they should send to the children's comic *Puck*. "We could say we'd misread the title."

But Europe was on the edge of the abyss; neither Vernon nor Dylan was ever to be so carefree again.

Chapter 7

CHANGES

Wait for no second Spring in Bishopston Valley.
Once, once only it breaks. – V. W.

Two weeks before war was declared *The Map of Love* was published.
Dylan sent Vernon an advance copy. "My book couldn't have come
out in a viler month," he wrote. "…This war, trembling over on the edge
of Laugharne, fills me with such horror and terror and lassitude…" Not
only had he achieved a precarious happiness, as he told his father, 'out of
nothing', but he foresaw – no-one more clearly, in spite of his youth – the
tide of suffering that was to overwhelm the world.

On the 3rd of September, Thomas Taig, of the Department of English
at the University College of Swansea, and the producer of *The Influences*,
drove Vernon to Laugharne.

There were a lot of soldiers in the pub there, and some deserters
were drinking with the escorts who had come to collect them
and who had practically decided to desert too. The room in
the pub on that evening was one of the most confused rooms I
have ever seen. Outside it was the hill, Laugharne Castle, and
the landscape that Dylan would write about in 'Over Sir John's
Hill' and the last poems. He loved it, and he hated everything
to do with the war; and he knew that very soon he would have
to decide whether to register as a conscientious objector or for
military service. Dylan did, in fact, make this decision in a rather
unexpected way. He felt that it would be best and most logical
to be a conscientious objector, but he had to attend a tribunal
for objectors in Wales as a witness. As each objector came

forward, he was asked on what grounds he objected to military service, and in each case a mean little voice answered "'ligious.' Each was then asked what he was prepared to do, and each answered, in an even meaner little voice, 'Nothing.' When Dylan left this court he felt that one door was closed to him, and later, when his own turn came, he confessed to me that he had signed for the army, but as a never-fighter. "Talk about the lads of the land," he said, describing his call-up. "Most of them were twisted with rheumatism, and none looked under fifty. The man next to me said he would join the Navy as he wanted to fly. He was classified D4, and I was C3."

C3 meant that, if Dylan were ever called up, it would be for clerical work or in some other non-combatant role. It is interesting to speculate what he would have made of Army life, and, indeed, what the Army would have made of him. Plenty of men, as unfitted for practical life, were blundering and staggering through life in the Services. They were generally looked after by a mate or group of mates, they had all meals provided, and their laundry was done, their hair cut, teeth inspected and health taken care of. They had a regular, if small, wage, a regular travel pass to see their families, and their wives received some money, too. Dylan would certainly have been popular for his wit and his fondness for beer, and would never have had to be alone at night. Would it have made a difference to his subsequent life? Who knows?

During the period of the 'phoney war', the Bank would not release Vernon; although he registered for call-up, he was put on Deferred Service. So, for a little while longer, life went on much as usual. Keidrych Rhys, the editor of *Wales*, was married in Llanstephan at the beginning of October, and Dylan was to be his best man.

"Have you got a respectable suit you can lend me, or, rather, trust me with?" he wrote to Vernon. "I'll return it, unegged, straight after the wedding – the next day; really, I can't undress in the church porch." Vernon sent him, as a gift, not a loan, his last year's bank suit. "It's grand of you to let me keep it," wrote Dylan. "I am now ready for all sartorial occasions, so long as at some of them I can appear in jersey and corduroys and at others in a smart brown suit, slightly open in the middle, with its pockets full of rice." Incidentally, this must have been the only time that Dylan actually succeeded in fulfilling his role as best man. At Constantine FitzGibbon's wedding he turned up only for the reception, and at Vernon's he did not turn up at all.

Nor did the war stop the reading and writing of poetry. Vernon had stayed at Laugharne in June, and had recited to Dylan, 'when we were walking down a hill', the great Yeats poems that appeared posthumously in the *London Mercury: Lapis Lazuli, The Statues, Long-legged Fly* and *News For the Delphic Oracle*. In November, Dylan asked Vernon to send him copies of them for a proposed reading to the English Club at Cambridge, together with some poems of his own. Vernon had also introduced Dylan to John Crowe Ransom, both agreeing that they liked *Captain Carpenter* and *Judith of Bethulia* better than any others.

Vernon was at this time working on his poem, *The Windows*, later printed in *The Ballad of the Mari Lwyd* as *The Windows of Breath*. Dylan did not care for it; he called it 'a serious failure – I mean it is a serious poem which fails,' and (using its own words) 'a camphored elegy.' Vernon took criticism far more aggressively than Dylan did, but he largely rewrote the poem. Dylan himself was working on *Once Below a Time*. This was almost the only one of his poems which Vernon did not care for; he thought it cocky and flippant without being witty, and he really disliked the tarted-up cliché, even when it occurred in a poem as beautiful as *Fern Hill*. What he did like was the Nansen line in the poem:

Cold Nansen's beak on a boat full of gongs.

Nansen was an old hero of his, and the subject of a poem written at Repton which had won him a prize.

Dylan, Caitlin and Llewellyn spent the Christmas of 1939 at Bishopston. Dylan wrote on December 13, "What do I want for Christmas? Oh, that's nice. I want a war-escaper – a sort of ladder, I think, attached to a balloon – or a portable ivory tower, or a new plush womb to escape back into.

Vernon and Dylan at Laugharne, Autumn 1939
'...many, many thanks for the supersmart suit in which no moth-holes could be seen...'

Or a lotion for invisibility." He might write comically about the war, but he was appalled by what he called 'world lunacy'. Perhaps he could be serious about its horror only in verse. That Christmas, he told Vernon that he felt he must continue to celebrate in his poetry:

> the praise of everything that war crushed and rejected. He set himself to re-state the holiness of life in the scenery of Hell and irrational death... the changes he made were, as in all the late poetry, away from ironical statement and in the direction of religious truth.

When the family left Bishopston, to stay with Caitlin's mother in Ringwood, Dylan was working on *There Was a Saviour*. This, a poem about invasion, was the first of the magnificent war poems, which afterwards included *A Refusal to Mourn, Holy Spring, Ceremony After a Fire Raid* and *Among Those Killed in the Dawn Raid Was a Man Aged a Hundred.* The later ones are among the great war poems of any language. Of *There Was a Saviour,* Vernon wrote:

> This was really the first of the entirely assonantal poems. Dylan had from the first preferred the method of mixing rhymes and half-rhymes, but his test for a rhyme was that you should not expect it. He certainly did not like writing in unrhymed form. He welcomed obstacles and difficulties. But he also did not like, as he once told me, finding his rhymes labelled for him like the stations on railway tickets. He wanted to preserve a strictness of choice in language with which direct rhyme sometimes interfered. So he resorted to assonance and dissonance and built his stanzas on a fabric of exact language in which the line-endings were musically and mathematically balanced, and enhanced, rather than reproduced, the sound that had gone before.

In answer to Vernon's appreciation of the poem, Dylan wrote in March 1940, "I'm so glad you liked (it), that you thought it was one of my best... About line 3 of the last verse, you're right as can be, and somehow I must make 'death' the second word... Your criticism's always terribly suggestive, and in that particular 'death line' you showed quite clearly to me the one big misbalance in the poem. Ta." The 'death line' was originally:

Deaths of the only ones, our never found.

It was reworked as:

Brave deaths of only ones but never found.

The first draft of Vernon's long poem *Ballad of the Mari Lwyd* was finished in March 1940. Vernon wrote of it with great excitement to Dylan, but waited until Dylan and Caitlin were again in Bishopston to show it to him. They were there temporarily in May because of a crisis in their financial affairs. "I've had to sneak my family away from our home in Carmarthenshire," he wrote to Stephen Spender, "because we could no longer obtain any credit and it was too awful to try to live there, among dunning and suspicion, from hand to mouth, when I knew the

Worm's Head. Dylan, Wyn Lewis and Vernon

hand would nearly always be empty."

Dreary though it must have been for Dylan and Caitlin to live with, and on, his parents, it must have been a month of unmitigated bliss for Vernon. One day, Wyn Lewis drove them to Rhossili. They walked out along the Worm, a rocky promontory jutting out from Rhossili beach (scene of *Extraordinary Little Cough*), and were nearly cut off by the tide. Dylan and Vernon were walking some way behind Wyn and Caitlin when they first became aware that the pools between the Worm and the mainland were filling up. Wyn and Caitlin began to run and managed to jump to dry land, but Dylan, podgy and soon beginning to pant, became almost frantic at the prospect of spending eight hours on the Worm while Caitlin was alone on the beach with the ravishingly handsome Wyn. Knee-deep in waves and completely breathless, he was finally dragged by Vernon up the sand. When they had climbed back up to the Downs, each of them took a photograph of the other three: Dylan still looks serious, almost sullen, at his escape from jealousy.

It was during this period too that Vernon, Dylan and Caitlin went to a performance of *The Marriage of Figaro* at the Empire Theatre. While they were waiting for the opera to begin, Dylan quoted to Vernon the first two lines of a new poem, which he was going to call *Deaths and Entrances*:

> On almost the incendiary eve
> Of several near deaths

He said that he was going to call his next book by the same title, "because that is all I ever write about or want to write about." Later, in November, he brought the poem to Heatherslade and spent the evening completing it. The final line, 'Looms the last Samson of your zodiac', was based on a suggestion of Vernon's, and Dylan always remained uncertain about it, 'Because zodiac is a Watkins word, not a Thomas word.' The last lines originally contained a hyena image suggested by one of his favourite passages from *Nightwood*.

> For the lover, it is the night into which his beloved goes... that
> destroys his heart; he wakes her suddenly, only to look the hyena
> in the face that is her smile, as she leaves that company...

Dylan was not satisfied with the hyena ending either:

> His exposition of the ending was elaborate and detailed. He did not write it down, but he spoke of all the accumulated forces of the projected words, and the weight they had to carry. I still have a work-sheet on which he jotted down some of the images which finally composed the last stanza, and it brings that particular evening to life more clearly than any photograph could have done.

That evening, and others like it, came to an end. In June, when Dylan was, briefly, back in Laugharne, he wrote:

> What a lot of pities we never could arrange longer and noisier evenings, noisy with our own poems, and even with poor Yeats's or done Pound's... But we had our moments, I heard *Baille's Strand* and two, at least, fine ones of your own, we heard *Figaro* and "I am," very very high up in the Empire roof, Beethoven accompanied our croquet, you nearly caught us napping on the Worm – and what would a stranger, hearing suddenly, make of that?

There was one more visit to Bishopston before Dylan's parents left it for ever, but, between this one and that one, the 'blood-dimmed tide' had rolled in. France had fallen in June, the Battle of Britain was fought in August, in the autumn, the blitzes began. By December, invasion seemed likely. Dylan, though terrified, was not a coward. Dr Daniel Jones said of him, "He dreaded and avoided pain, but actually sought... a confrontation with injury or danger." He never avoided London during the bombing raids, not even during the later V1 and V2 attacks. But for the time being, he was safe in John Davenport's house in Marshfield, near Chippenham, spending the summer with other artists and musicians. "Davenport and I are writing a fantastic thriller together, so I haven't done a poem for a long time although there are 2 I want to write badly: both nightmares, I'm afraid. Oh Europe etcetera please do be bettera."

Francis Labeyrie, who had been married in London in 1939, had, of course, returned to France on the outbreak of war. At first, communications were normal, and Vernon was able to send him each issue of *Life and Letters Today* as it came out, with letters that always contained news of Dylan. In September 1939, Francis wrote from Bayonne, in the Basses- Pyrenees, "I was glad to read *The Ballad of the Rough Sea* and also Dylan's story, *Extraordinary Little Cough*, which seems to me very different from what I read of him before. I liked it 'a lot'. You will be good to send me the next copy… *Life and Letters* is a friendly thing when it comes, and one of the rare things now that keep you from losing heart." And after receiving the December issue: "Dylan's story stirs up lots of good memories of him in my mind, extravagant walks we had together in Swansea, visits to people living near the Docks, his talk and lots of eccentric things so good to remember; personally that's what I like best in his autobiographical stories. I liked the previous one better than *The Fight*, though."

By January 1940, Francis was in the army, and remembering Dylan's horror of weapons, he wrote, "As I am the tallest in our section, I have been entrusted with the '*fusilmitrailleur*' (light M G). Tell Dylan it fires 600 shots a minute!" Vernon managed to get a copy of *Portrait of the Artist as a Young Dog* to him before the fall of France.

"I went to Paris," Francis wrote, "and spent my time in the train reading *One Warm Saturday, The Peaches* and *Where Tawe Flows*. It is a very entertaining book… It's more easy to apprehend to one remembering Dylan's wisecracks in actual life and speech. I am glad to recognise in it bits of scenery I know, the Grammar School, the Singleton, and the Welsh too."

But the 'bits of scenery' Francis knew, among them the Grammar School, were soon only a memory. "I can't imagine Gower bombed," wrote Dylan from Marshfield. "High explosives at Pennard. Flaming onions over Pwlldu. And Union Street ashen. This is all too near."

Vernon had hoped to fly to Paris, to attend the christening of Francis's daughter Danielle, but the Germans were marching on Paris, and attacking it from the air. Later, he was to write *The Broken Sea,* a poem in which grief for his god-daughter, 'born in a wailing time', mingles with grief for the loss of his past and his friends.

> I was going to fly to your christening to give you a cup.
> Here, like Andersen's tailor, I weave the invisible thread.
> The burnt-out clock of St. Mary's has come to a stop,
> And the hand still points to the figure that beckons the house-stoned dead.

> Child shades of my ignorant darkness, I mourn that moment alive
> Near the glow-lamped Eumenides' house overlooking the ships in flight,
> Where Pearl White focussed our childhood, near the foot of Cwmdonkin Drive,
> To a figment of crime stampeding in the posters' wind-blown blight.

> I regret the broken Past, its prompt and punctilious cares,
> All the villainies of the fire-and-brimstone-visited town.
> I miss the painter of limbo at the top of the fragrant stairs,
> The extravagant hero of night, his iconoclastic frown.

But Danielle's father could not read the poem, for silence had fallen on France.

Dylan and Caitlin spent a long time at Bishopston, from Christmas onwards, more poverty-stricken than ever, and in disgrace with his parents because he had lost his ration-books. "We've been cooped up here, in little, boiling rooms, quite broke," he wrote to John Davenport in January. "Today the pipes burst, and Caitlin, in a man's hat, has been running all day with a mop from W. C. to flooded parlour, while I've been sitting down trying to write a poem about a man who fished with a woman for bait and caught a horrible collection." (Dylan would have thought his own task incomparably the more difficult of the two.)

This poem was *Ballad of the Long-Legged Bait*, written when Vernon was seeing Dylan as often as three or four times a week – as often as he could, indeed, knowing that he would soon be called up.

> I saw this poem grow from its first fifteen lines through all
> the stages of its composition. He wrote the four-lined verses
> in pairs. The poem is full of visual imagery. It was so much a

visual poem that he made a coloured picture for it which he pinned on the wall of his room, a picture of a woman lying at the bottom of the sea. She was a new Lorelei revealing the pitfalls of destruction awaiting those who attempted to put off the flesh.

Dylan also borrowed Vernon's typewriter, 'for short, irregular periods,' he wrote rather aggrievedly to Davenport. He can hardly have been aware what a stringent test of Vernon's love for him it was, that he had been allowed to borrow it at all. Until about 1934, Vernon wrote all his poems in manuscript; but after being given a typewriter, he was rapidly converted. He felt that the poem could only be surveyed impersonally in print. Dylan felt so too. "Don't be too harsh to these poems until they're typed," he had written in March 1938. "I always think typescript lends some sort of certainty: at least, if the things are bad then they appear to be bad with conviction; in ordinary mss. they look as if they might be altered at any moment." At this time, Vernon often made even first drafts of a new poem in typescript, and so, to be without it, even for 'short, irregular periods', must have been a real deprivation for him. As soon as his initial training in the Royal Air Force was over and he was posted to a station, he retrieved his typewriter from Pennard, and thereafter it went with him until his demobilisation.

In three night-raids, in February, the centre and some suburbs of Swansea were destroyed by fire-bombs. Vernon, in the Home Guard, watched the glare of the burning town from the heights of Cefn Bryn. Dylan, meeting a friend in the ruins of the Market, said with tears, "Our Swansea is dead."

It was the beginning of the end of their Swansea past. Because of the raids, Dylan's parents prepared to move from Bishopston to safer Carmarthenshire. In May, Dylan and Caitlin were back in Laugharne, staying in the Castle with Frances Hughes while Richard was at sea. Fred Janes, Dan Jones and Tom Warner were in the Army, John Prichard in the Navy.

Vernon had applied for the Field Security Police (!) but he had been turned down because he could not ride a motor-cycle; when he tried, he went round and round in ever decreasing circles until he and the motor-bike fell over together. Dylan did not care for the armed forces. "I'm glad you wrote, telling the officials you can only just turn on a bathroom tap. Be a censor: pry and erase. Don't be a cyclist or a parachutist or a mine-tester or the first man on the *very* edge of Dover cliffs."

At about this time, Dylan was working on a novel, of which he had read the first two chapters to Vernon while he was still at Bishopston. They had discussed possible titles. *The Skins* was not quite right; *A Trader in Skins* or *A Traveller in Skins* might do. Dylan had finally decided on *Adventures in the Skin Trade*. Now, from Laugharne Castle, he wrote,

"My prose-book's going well, but I dislike it. It's the only really dashed-off piece of work I remember doing. I've done 10,000 words already. It's indecent and trivial, sometimes funny, sometimes mawkish, and always badly written, which I do not mind so much." A week later, he wrote, "My novel blathers on. It's a mixture of Oliver Twist, Little Dorrit, Kafka, Beachcomber, and three-adjectives-a-penny belly-churning Thomas, the Rimbaud of Cwmdonkin Drive."

Not long after this, Vernon was in Laugharne for a weekend:

I was there when a London publisher's letter arrived, expressing disappointment in the opening chapters of the novel. It was not, ran the letter, the great, serious autobiographical work to which they had looked forward so long. The manuscript would be returned, and it was hoped that he would offer them something autobiographical, but different, at a later date. Dylan re-read the letter with amused indignation. He was hard up, and a letter of acceptance would have been far more satisfactory. He protested to me that, whatever the publisher said, he thought the book entertaining, and he would not write any sort of solemn rhetoric. At this time he used to write mainly in the afternoon, and after lunch he disappeared, and showed me a new part he had written when he emerged for tea. It covered about a page and was extremely funny.

Dylan talked to Vernon a great deal about the plot of this book.

It was to show what happened to a person, like himself, who took life as it came. This central character, Samuel Bennet, would attract adventures to him by his own unadventurous stillness and natural acceptance of every situation. He would accept life, like a baby who had been given self-dependence. He would have no money, no possessions, no extra clothes, no civilised bias. And life would come to him... There was to be a succession of scenes, each being an allegorical layer of life, and at the end of the story the character would be stripped of all illusion, naked at last. It would be in one way a journey through the Inferno of London, but it would also be a comedy. There is no doubt that, beneath the absurdity of situation which would provide furniture for the scenes, lay the influence and sense of tragedy of Webster's *Duchess of Malfi* and Marlowe's *Doctor Faustus*. Had the novel been finished, it is unlikely that the comic central character of the first chapters would not have been revealed as also a tragic figure.

The novel never was finished; it has only three chapters. What was the 'unseen obstacle to his imagination'? Vernon said, in his *Afterword* to the Signet edition, that "the pressure of the anarchy of war itself and the vision of distorted London had taken the place of his half-fictional vision and compelled his imagination forward..." Perhaps; but some chapters were written after he had experienced the reality of bombed cities; and, in any case, Dylan sent the manuscript to a publisher in January 1944 apparently with every intention of completing it. I believe that the real difficulty was the intrinsically impossible premise on which the plot rested; and that this was the story of the dichotomy in Dylan's own life. If a baby were given self-dependence, he would die, because he has no ability to use it. If he could use it, he wouldn't be a baby. This was essentially an autobiographical work, but its central problem could be solved in art no more than it could be in life. Dylan longed to be Samuel Bennet, with freedom but no responsibility; but, unlike his anti-hero, he could not simply remain where he was. Time and life carried him forward, the split in his nature always widening. Dr Daniel Jones says, "I cannot imagine how these two parts of his personality could be integrated and survive as one.

Meanwhile, Vernon did what he could to shore up the family's precarious life by continually responding to Dylan's entreaties for money. "If you ever have 5 shillings you hate, I shan't..." "If you do have a tiny bit to spare, whether it clinks or tinkles, let alone rustles, *do* send it, Vernon... Anything, bled boy, leper, from a penny to a pound." "See if you can squeeze another drop from your borrowed-to-death body." But it was pouring water into sand.

In the Spring of 1941, T. S. Eliot had accepted Vernon's first book of poems for Faber and Faber, although he did not approve of the title *Ballad of the Mari Lwyd*. "It's dollars to dimes," he wrote, "that everyone outside Wales will call it *The Ballad of the Marie Lloyd*. She was a great woman, and deserving such a tribute, but here it would be misleading." Vernon finally settled on a title which Dylan did not care for. "Faber's are bringing out Vernon's poems this year," he wrote to Davenport. I'm very glad. Provisionally titled *Gratitude of a Leper*, though I'm not quite sure myself."

"Any more about your leprous collection?" he asked Vernon in May 1941. "Perhaps the volume should be surgically bound. I do hope it comes out this summer, just before the gas." In fact it was published in October, under its original title, after an unexpected note from Eliot saying, "I hope it will not grieve you to return to your first love." (The *Leper* title was, of course, a reference to the New Testament story of the one leper out of ten who returned to give thanks to Christ for his healing.)

Ballad of the Mari Lwyd was pretty well received by the critics. It is difficult now to remember, or imagine, the enormous cachet derived from being a Faber poet. It is even more difficult to envisage, without actually looking at old newspapers and magazines, the really colossal amount of space devoted to reviews. The *T L S* gave it a 'Recommended' headline and two columns, referring to the originality of the poet's imagination and the potency of his rhythm and imagery. Sheila Shannon, in the *Spectator*, reviewed it with Walter de la Mare's *Bells and Grass*, and spoke of it as, "a remarkable collection of poems, with original and splendid melodies." All the Welsh papers were delighted to find a new Welsh poet, and the *Herald of Wales* gave him three page-length columns, with an amount of quotation that partially satisfied even Vernon, whose idea of a good review was one hundred per cent quotation.

He sent Dylan one of his author's copies, with, of course, an affectionate inscription; but Dylan did not acknowledge it, nor did he ever comment on the reviews. There was every excuse for him; he had at last found a regular job in London with Strand Films, but had not found a permanent place to live. For a short time, he and Caitlin lived in Hammersmith Terrace, then Caitlin was in a remote village, Talsarn in Cardiganshire, and Dylan commuted between there and London. Then, too, Vernon's long-deferred service came to an end in December 1941, and he was moving about to various training stations. Still, a note sent to Heatherslade would always have been forwarded.

Dylan evidently liked the *Ballad*. Constantine FitzGibbon says, "I do not remember him reading any of his contemporaries except Norman Cameron, and, much more, Vernon Watkins. He thought very highly of the *Ballad of the Mari Lwyd*, which I heard him read more than once." (No mean feat, by the way, if he read the whole poem, since it takes at least half an hour to read.) This was the beginning of a subtle change in their relationship. They had always been accustomed to discuss their own, or each other's poetry, with equal interest; but now there was no time (and no place) for the long, private sessions they had been used to. Doubtless, when Vernon was stationed at Uxbridge or Bletchley, and could get to London to see Dylan, there was a good deal of talk about poetry and poets, but it was no longer so personal; and, in any case, the meetings now often occurred with groups of other writers. There was no longer anyone with whom Vernon could discuss his poetry so intimately, and with such confidence in being understood, as with Dylan. He retreated into the poetic solitude he had known before he had met Dylan, but he never ceased to regret that those sessions,

> That strictest, lie-disrobing act
> Testing the poem read

were part of the past now, and would not come again.

Chapter 8

WARTIME

In a time of darkness the pattern of life is restored
By men who make all transience seem an illusion. – V. W.

It was more than a year before Dylan and Vernon met again. Vernon had elected to join the Royal Air Force Police, on the grounds that he would have to do some cooking if he became a cook, whereas he would not necessarily have to make arrests if he became a policeman. These were the only vacancies in the RAF at the time of his call-up, and he had no illusions about his competence in practical matters. In effect, he spent eighteen months in the RAF Police without making a single arrest. He did this by reading poetry in the waiting-room of railway stations, while the drunks and latecomers he was supposed to arrest ambled peacefully back to camp; by waiting round a corner until the combatants in a fight had sorted themselves out; by being absorbed in a book instead of sharply observing that people coming off leave booked in at the correct time, and in other ingenious ways.

Even patrolling the camp at night was not bad; he was on his own, and could compose poems in his head as he walked round the perimeter. (It was safest to do this, as if he penetrated the mysteries of the camp, he became irretrievably lost). Once, while he was waiting to go on guard, the Officer of the Watch, a child fresh from his OCTU, came trembling into the guardhouse to say that he could not think of a password for the night.

"It's all right, sir," Vernon comforted him. "It can be any word – any word at all."

"I know that," the officer said despairingly, sinking his head into his shaking hands, "but *I can't think of one.*"

Vernon always had a hearty appetite, and it was satisfactory, when he was on night duty, to be able to eat, not only the substantial meals provided for the guard, but also any of the meals for the day shift for which he could stay awake. For the first (and only) time in his life, he weighed more than twelve stones. He first became aware of this in the shower, when he found himself soaping a perceptible bosom, and a colleague in a neighbouring stall suggested that he should go to the Stores and indent for a brassiere.

There were some duties that were not pleasant and not to be avoided. One was lowering the flag at sunset; if it jammed half-way down, as it often did if Vernon was pulling the ropes, it was embarrassing to hear the flight-sergeant raving under his breath, while the bugler wearily played 'Lights Out' for the third time. Another job he greatly disliked was leaping on the running-board of a visiting VIP's car and directing his driver to wherever in the camp he wished to go. Vernon, who knew every rock and gully in Gower, seemed to be completely at sea anywhere else. He could never find his own way about the camp, and often ended up in the Ablutions when he wanted his own hut; so he would say smartly to the driver, "Turn left. Now, go straight on," until he passed someone from whom he could ask directions. Then, he would leap efficiently back, saying, "The camp has been completely reorganised recently, sir." He always avoided this duty if possible.

In early 1942, he was stationed at Uxbridge, where he came top of the Police Course, partly because of his very high marks in rifle and revolver shooting, but mainly because, whatever his lack of knowledge, he could answer questions in written exams in good English, while his course-mates, almost all far better policemen than he, found great difficulty in expressing themselves. The first time that he had a day pass, he arranged to meet Dylan in London, but had to be back in camp one minute before midnight.

He went up on the train, with two men from his hut. When they heard where he was going, they decided that, as they had never seen a famous poet, they would go with him. One was an East-end pub-owner, one a regular policeman from Norfolk. They liked Dylan, and Dylan liked them; so much that, when the pubs closed, he took them on to one of his clubs. When midnight struck, they were, like three Cinderellas, far from home. They had to hitch their way back to Uxbridge, and it was nearly two in the morning when they reached the camp. Two of them were pretty drunk, and the Norfolk policeman was almost incapable. They had had to hold him up between them after they climbed off the lorry. If they booked in at the camp entrance now, as they were supposed to do, not only would they all be put on a charge for overstaying their leave, but he would be on a further and more serious charge.

Vernon, used to swinging himself on to rock faces, was sure that he could break into camp, and persuaded the East-ender that he could do the same; the Norfolk policeman was lying blissfully unconscious on the ground in the pouring rain. After Herculean efforts, they managed to heave themselves and their passive companion over the fence, avoiding the guard patrol, and pussyfoot their way through the WAAF camp, forbidden to airmen, which was their point of entry. They dumped him silently on to his bed as dawn was breaking, leaving themselves about an hour to dry their soaked uniform and fake an entry in the booking-in book. The East-ender was immensely grateful and admiring. "Any time you come to my pub, drinks will be on the house," he declared. "I never had such a thing as a poet in there before, but now I don't care how many I have."

A few months later, Vernon left the police, with the amiable words, "I don't suppose I'll ever meet a bigger bunch of crooks," and was posted to Bletchley Park. Many books have been written about the Park since then, but none that even faintly conveys the atmosphere of the place. Many people roamed about its mansion, huts and blocks, almost all of them of superior education and intelligence, some of genius; but a great many of them were – well, strange, to put it mildly. When, years after leaving Bletchley, I read Constantine FiitzGibbon's account of Dylan's first idea for the plot of *Under Milk Wood*, I felt a sense of familiarity that I couldn't at first place.

> The village was declared insane, anti-social, dangerous. Barbed wire was strung about it, and patrolled by sentries, lest its dotty inhabitants infect the rest of the world with their feckless and futile way of life…The village is the only place that is left free in the whole world…This is not the concentration camp; the rest of the globe is the camp, is mad, and only this little place is sane, is happy.

The Park was certainly well fenced in and patrolled, and the outside world, as far as the inhabitants of Bletchley itself were concerned, probably thought its inhabitants dotty. They were, too, most of them; brilliant scholars, intellectuals and cryptographers, but indisputably dotty. They had lived in their own extraordinary worlds so long that Bletchley Park seemed quite normal to them. In the intervals between decoding, the scholars wrote their reviews; the chess-players queued to play twenty simultaneous games with Hugh Alexander, the British chess champion; the philosophers walked, arguing, round the lake where the body of a dead duckling swayed and floated; the musicians thumped and twanged; the novelists made, like Ibsen, card-indexes of their characters' lives. Although it was a railway junction, only a stray bomb or two dropped on its outskirts, abandoned by a fleeing German plane. It was an oasis of a kind of sanity in the madness of the warring world.

It suited Vernon. Here, nobody thought it strange to write poetry; other people wrote or reviewed it, and many people read it. There were tennis-courts and a permanent table-tennis tournament, and, not far away from his billet at New Bradwell, was Cowper's Olney, with the river for bathing or boating. Here, too, came Constantine FitzGibbon, Dylan's friend and future biographer; and in the Japanese section was Daniel Jones, one of Dylan's closest friends, who had known him since his schooldays, of whom Vernon had heard so much, and whom he now met for the first time.

Since we could never talk about our work outside our own section, gossip about personalities was part of the fabric of life at the Park. There were plenty of apocryphal stories about Captain Jones: how, on the final day of his Officers' Selection Course, a question was put to him by a Colonel of warlike aspect. "Officer-Cadet Jones, you are marching along a country road with a small detachment of men when suddenly enemy parachutists begin to land in a field to your left. At the same time a bus carrying civilians overturns and bursts into flame on the road before you. What is your course of action?"

Officer-Cadet Jones did not hesitate for a second. Springing to attention, he snapped, "I should give the order to fix bayonets and charge, sir!"

"Now, gentlemen," said the Colonel with satisfaction, turning to his fellow Selectors, "*that* is the sort of quick thinking that will win us the war."

Dylan particularly relished the story of the occasion when a formidable lady senior officer from the War Office, the Head of a Section which was in some ways the counterpart of Dan's Bletchley Park Section, in a rather slack interval, arrived for a consultation. The five or six members of the Section were refreshing themselves with a brisk paper-balls-and-rubber-bands battle, when she opened the door, earlier than had been expected, and stood majestically surveying the scene as paper balls struck and rebounded from her steely form.

"Captain Jones," she said, after a pregnant pause, "I do the same amount of work as you, with one assistant."

"Indeed," said Captain Jones, politely rising from his crouching position behind an overturned filing cabinet, "and how do you divide the work?"

Vernon had been admiring Dan by proxy, as it were, ever since he had heard of him from Dylan. Now he found a great deal more to admire in such a polymath. In spite of his immense knowledge and attainments, he was not conceited.

"Was that piece in a minor key?" Vernon asked him. "No, actually in the major," said Dan kindly. "*Nearly* right."

He was as much interested as Vernon in poetry, and much more knowledgeable about prose. He knew as many comic stories as Dylan, and many more languages than Vernon, who was fascinated by his descriptions of Chinese ideographs, particularly of the incredibly detailed verbs. Vernon especially liked 'to shell peas secretly at midnight', and would frequently speculate on the incidents which would lead one to use this verb. Once, when Dan had been visiting him at Stony Stratford, Vernon shouted as Dan climbed on to his homeward bus, "Come and have another midnight pea sometime!" The crowd waiting for the next bus were only too evidently not familiar with Chinese verbs. Vernon was rather good at causing multi-lingual misunderstandings. One crowded Saturday afternoon in Swansea, after trying in vain to attract the attention of the assistant in order to buy a copy of *Lettres Françaises*, he at last bawled over the head of the suddenly silenced purchasers, "Miss! Miss! I say, do you have French Letters here?"

Vernon and Dan were both fond of word games. They invented one of which the object was to compose a two-sentence scene or playlet, in which the two lines should sound identical but have different meanings. But in order to explain the two sentences, some sort of preface was necessary. The longer and more complex the build-up and the shorter the two phrases, the more triumphant was the perpetrator. It grew out of a playlet in which the opening scene showed King Canute majestically addressing the ocean with the words, 'Obey, O bay!' His daughter, seeing the royal feet washed by the disobedient waves, sensibly cautioned him, "No, pa King; no parking." Later the game rose to such heights as:

Scene: a concert hall. On the platform, a symphony orchestra is tuning up. A foreign music critic, conspicuous for his un-English clothes and his extravagant gestures of disapproval during the performance, leaps to his feet as the music comes to an end in a welter of discords. "Symphony," he shrieks. "Sim fonny!" Or: a variety show is in progress. An acrobat is balancing on various objects, beginning with large beach-balls and continuing with ever smaller spheres, such as footballs, melons, grapefruit, and oranges. Finally, to the accompaniment of a drum-roll, he balances on a crab-apple. A member of the audience, convinced that he can do even better, shouts, "Encore ! On core!"

Flight-Sergeant Watkins and Captain Jones very occasionally went to London, using day-passes, to see Dylan, who, in the autumn of 1942, had found a place for himself and Caitlin to live, in Wentworth Studios, Manresa Road, Chelsea. In *My Friend Dylan Thomas*, Dr Jones has described these wartime meetings:

> I would have been wise not to seek Dylan out at all during those short leaves from Bletchley. It was impossible to detach him from a new circle of acquaintances, some of whom treated me with less than courtesy... At the same time, Dylan himself seemed different. He was now a famous man and often the centre of an admiring circle. I am ready to admit that in my feelings towards the closest of the sycophants there may have been a touch of jealousy as I awkwardly shuffled about on the periphery of that charmed circle, but far stronger than this was the sense that Dylan had become remote. I suspect that if some proportion of the small amount of time I had for each London visit could have been spent alone with Dylan or with Dylan and two or three really close friends, any impression made on him by the insinuations of his new acquaintances would have vanished, and my feeling of the distance between us would have vanished too.

I think that Dan misunderstood Dylan's motives and behaviour on these London visits. He was, in any case, always jealous of his importance in Dylan's life, having for all their adolescence been not only Dylan's greatest friend, but also his mentor, being two years older and many years more knowledgeable. But, of course, as Dylan became a well-known poet and less of a provincial boy, this relationship had to change. Dan did not like this; he wanted things to stay the same, with Dylan admiring him as he had always done. Now, Dylan had many admirers of his own, and also made new friends in the broadcasting and film industries, about which Dan knew nothing whatever. After the war, they met infrequently, and, as Caitlin pointed out, usually reverted to their boyhood, playing French Cricket and pushing each other about with unmeaning insults, as they used to do. It was, perhaps, the only way they could remain friends. Dylan knew nothing about Dan's music and cared less, and Dan could certainly no longer help Dylan with his poems.

Vernon did not mind Dylan's new status. He liked to talk to anyone who admired Dylan, and was always pleased to listen to Dylan talking. He managed, too, quite often, to have some time alone with Dylan, or with Dylan and a friend such as Constantine FitzGibbon or Phil Lindsay. He had, in any case, a singular lack of jealousy in his nature, but there was one habit of Dylan's that greatly embarrassed him. Dylan would walk up to the biggest man in uniform in the pub and insult him, his country and the war so grossly that, almost inevitably, a fight developed. John Prichard told me that he had once been walking past the Eight Bells, when the door opened and Dylan came rolling out, followed by Caitlin, who said despairingly, "If only Dylan would just once pick on a *little* man!" But, of course, Caitlin was often the cause of these fights. Angered by the crowd surrounding Dylan and the lack of attention paid to her, she would flirt outrageously with someone in uniform till Dylan noticed. Vernon never knew whether he was supposed to go to Dylan's aid in the fights, which his sense of justice told him were entirely the fault of the aggressor. "Dylan," he said, "was the most aggressive pacifist I have ever seen," who "resented the smug talk he heard about the war and… did not disguise his resentment." In a short piece in *Encounter*, in 1956, Vernon wrote:

> The poet of apparently destructive force was certainly the most ethical, the most constant of companions. He did not believe there was such a thing as a comfortable conscience. Where he found that people around him were becoming puppets of self-satisfaction he did frequently break up the ground on which they

stood. Such moods of violent exasperation coloured the false impression of a romantic poet rather than a true apprehension of the ethical witness. For a witness he always was, and the severest witness of his own behaviour. He tried to adapt his behaviour to his company. Considering each person to be an entire world, he was willing to go a long way with any man in his imagination to explore that world; but a world where Mammon took the place of God never failed to bore and disgust him. His instinct in conversation was to give, and to give prodigiously, and it was also to draw out ideas, to expose fallacies...

Dylan was not only courageous in attacking, if attack he must, the strongest and most formidable man in any company (and I have to agree with Vernon that it was never until he had listened to that man expressing smug, racist or destructive sentiments), he was also brave in air-raids. His courage was the true courage of the terror-stricken:

> He hated being in his house if there were an air-raid, but he did not mind the raid if he were in a pub. That is to say, he minded it terribly, but he felt he was in the right place.

Vernon was staying in Manresa Road when a very bad air-raid began, just after they had come back from the pub. They crouched under the heavy table, which shook with Dylan's shivering. Vernon, to calm him, began talking of his belief in the immortality of the soul. Dylan, still trembling, made a reply which Vernon never forgot:

> In London, when the blinds were drawn
> Blackening a barbarous sky,
> He plucked, beneath the accusing beams,
> The mote out of his eye.
> In the one death his eye discerned
> The death all deaths must die.
>
> 'My immortality,' he said,
> 'Now matters to my soul
> Less than the deaths of others.'

Not by the wars of human minds
Nor by the jealous word
Nor by the black of London's blinds
Or coffin's rattling cord,
But by the stillness of that voice
The picture is restored.

'The death all deaths must die' is a reference to the line, 'After the first death there is no other,' in *A Refusal to Mourn the Death by Fire of a Child in London*. This magnificent poem was sent to Vernon in the same envelope as *The Conversation of Prayer* and *A Winter's Tale*.

Another blitz incident was one remembered by Dylan and used in several ways in his comic articles. Dylan and Vernon were in a taxi going down Regent Street, when a flying bomb cut out directly overhead. It came to earth some little distance away, and as the taxi drove on through dust and smoke, Dylan said in a trembling voice, "Wasn't it funny? I was sure we were going to be killed, and all I could think of was that I hoped I'd be blown to bits, because I didn't want my body found with *Reveille* open at the pin-ups page."

"I should have been all right," Vernon said complacently, "because I always carry Kierkegaard in my pocket." Dylan was very much amused, and Vernon's remark turned up years later in *A Visit to America*:

Of the lecture he (the visiting poet) remembers little but the applause and maybe two questions: 'Is it true that young English intellectuals are *really* psychological?' or 'I always carry Kierkegaard in my pocket. What do you carry?'

In his edition of Dylan's letters, Vernon says that he lost all the letters that came between August 1941 and July 1944. But he points out that

The years, in fact, which are not here represented by letters were years when we saw each other more often than at any time since he left Swansea. The letters that came then were often mere notes arranging to meet, the discussion of poems being postponed until the meeting, when the exact analysis of his written self-criticism gave way to the concise and lightning judgments of his conversation.

If Vernon says he lost some letters, then those letters were lost, because his memory (always marvellously good for anything that interested him '– 'old Datas Watkins', as Dylan called him) would never be at fault in anything that concerned Dylan. If that is so, then it is a great loss to British epistolary literature. But it surprises me, since every fragment of Dylan's handwriting was precious to Vernon. After the war, in 1955, one letter, as Vernon discreetly puts it, 'disappeared'. He was giving a talk on Dylan's poetry, and afterwards, rather unwisely, as I could not help thinking at the time, he spread out all the letters on a small table, for those who were interested to inspect. Still, the audience was a professional one whom he had every reason to trust, since some were friends and most of the others were their colleagues. All the same... when I checked the letters at home, a single sheet with a draft of *There Was a Saviour* was missing, and so was the 'short one, almost entirely personal', which is referred to in the Introduction to the *Letters*, and which will be dealt with in the next chapter.

Chapter 9

THE WAR ENDS

Memory plays tricks with imagination and imagination with memory. – V. W.

On the 27th of July 1944, Dylan wrote to Vernon, "I didn't think it was so long since we saw each other, or since I wrote to you," and ending, "Write very soon, please, and tell me everything."

'Everything' included the fact that Vernon was engaged, and wanted Dylan to be best man at his wedding in October. Dylan immediately answered with a short, affectionate message of congratulation; in effect, a beautiful little prose poem. Vernon treasured this greatly, and its disappearance grieved him deeply. It was, unfortunately, a gift for a thief, being on a slip of paper rather smaller than a postcard, and having no address or superscription, but written in Dylan's eminently recognisable handwriting.

We were both in the Sergeants' Mess at Bletchley, since Vernon was a Flight-Sergeant and I a Sergeant – through no particular merit or qualifications of our own, but because all Air Force code-breakers were promoted. One morning in September, Vernon showed me a letter from Dylan with an enclosure. This was, Dylan said, "a month and a bit premature." The enclosure was his birthday poem for 1944, *Poem in October*. It had originally been a birthday poem for 1941, with the first line:

It was my twenty-seventh year to heaven.

I read it in the noisy Mess, with the wireless playing *You Are My Sunshine,* with billiard balls being knocked about, with coffee-cups clinking, and it was a staggeringly beautiful poem. I knew nothing about the work of

Dylan Thomas, and Vernon employed our free time in reading aloud some of his poems, and all the stories from *Portrait of the Artist as a Young Dog.* A generation that has come to accept Dylan as a great poet, but a poet in text books and examination syllabuses, must find it difficult to understand the freshness, the explosive originality of his prose, and the majesty and exaltation of his poetry, after the political and sociological poetry of the thirties. My student friends from Oxford asked me, unbelievingly, if I were really going to marry someone who was a friend of this famous figure, and they clamoured to be invited to the wedding. We were, in fact, constrained by time, money, the difficulties of travel and wartime in our entertaining of guests, and able to invite only our parents and Vernon's sisters. (My fourteen-year-old brother had received his invitation with a horrified stare and a definite, *"Not on your life!"*). Vernon had not, in fact, thought of inviting Caitlin, since she was at that time living in Newquay with the children; but Dylan had written, "… of course we are coming to your marriage, in our brightest colours."

Vernon and I had been able to get a 48-hour leave pass at the same time, and had arranged for the wedding to take place on October 2nd, in the chapel of St. Bartholomew the Great. The wedding party was to lunch in a private room in the Charing Cross Hotel. A close friend of ours at Bletchley happened to be strolling down Regent Street as Vernon came out of a florist's, bearing a great sheaf of long-stemmed, golden roses for the altar. "You look as though you're going to a wedding," said the friend.

"I am," replied Vernon. "Why don't you come?" Not realising that it was Vernon's own wedding he was being invited to, and ready for any celebration, dear Brian Verdier (now long dead) happily came with Vernon.

Back at the hotel, I had problems of my own. As I couldn't invite my numerous aunts and uncles, I had arranged that a telegram explaining the circumstances should be delivered at my grandmother's house on the actual morning of the 2nd. But one aunt had, by the skin of her teeth, caught a train from Birmingham, and arrived at the hotel, triumphant and yet shamefaced, as she knew what a dreadful family crisis she would cause; and, indeed, my mother was in the process of explaining her frightful misdemeanours to her when I arrived. I was too preoccupied with this incident to notice that the best man had not yet turned up. I had other apprehensions, too. My father was not by any means a conventional man, and would have got on well with Dylan, had he met him in a pub; but he would have expected proper, conventional behaviour at his only daughter's wedding. And from what I had heard, Dylan's behaviour was often very far from conventional, and Caitlin's was really unpredictable. So, I was relieved that their arrival, in their brightest clothes, was delayed. If we could just sit straight down to lunch, and then go immediately to the church, I thought, things could not go far wrong.

Vernon, however, became increasingly anxious, hurrying up and down between the reception desk and the lunch-room, but was reassured at one o'clock by a message from the secretary at Gryphon Films, which said that she had just seen Mr Thomas into a taxi, and that he would be at the hotel in a short time. A plate and some beer were put aside for him, and Vernon ate his lunch, feeling reassured. At two o'clock, we had to leave for the church, and Dylan had still not arrived. Messages to come straight to the church were left at the desk, but it was clear that Dylan had abandoned the taxi for some reason, and Vernon, knowing his dilatory habits, began to fear that he would turn up too late. It still did not occur to him that Dylan would not turn up at all.

The church of St. Bartholomew the Great lay open to the mellow autumn sunshine; only the Lady Chapel, with the golden roses on the altar, still had a roof. We waited there until the clergyman said that he had another wedding soon and could wait no longer. Brian Verdier, who had not yet recovered from his amazement that the wedding he had been invited to was Vernon's own, almost in a trance, was persuaded up to the altar-rail, to take the part of best man; and so we were married. Vernon was a profoundly religious man, and the marriage service meant a great deal to him; but Dylan's absence left a blank in his heart. Back at the hotel, he looked anxiously for a message, but there was none. It was not until our train pulled out of St. Pancras station that he sank back in his seat and said, "That's the end of Dylan, as far as I'm concerned." I said that perhaps the taxi had broken down or been involved in an accident. "The only possible excuse," Vernon said bitterly, "is that he's paralysed from the neck down, or dead."

Nevertheless, he waited anxiously for a letter from Dylan. When none came, I suggested that he might write himself, but this he absolutely refused to do. He must have thought that, if Dylan cared so little about his feelings that he could neither take the trouble to come to the wedding, nor apologise for not having done so, there could be little point in any longer thinking of him as a friend. It was a bitter blow.

And yet, when Dylan's letter did arrive, four weeks later on the 30th October, all bitterness disappeared instantly. "You see," he said triumphantly, "it wasn't his fault at all. He couldn't help it — there was nothing he could do." He so much wanted to believe this (he was in any case prone to believe anything that was told him; he was an easy man to deceive) that I kept my own misgivings to myself. The letter sounded spurious to me. In any case, there was that telephone call to the Charing Cross Hotel, saying that Dylan was in the taxi. Although he had been told the name of the church, there was never any question that he should go there at one o'clock. It was clear that he had abandoned the taxi, or told it to go somewhere else. Indeed, Paul Ferris, that biographer whose researches (unlike those of many other writers on Dylan) can always be trusted to be accurate, says that Dylan was, at roughly the time that the wedding was taking place, in the office of a London publisher, being paid £10 of a £50 advance on a projected work — which, incidentally, was never written.

So, why did Dylan fail to turn up to Vernon's wedding? Was it, as I once thought, that he found formal occasions, meeting strangers, too frightening? Did he get out of the taxi to have one last drink at a pub, and delay until it was too late? Did he just dismiss the whole thing as a bore, and go to wheedle some money from Gottlieb? I don't know. What is obvious is that his letter of apology is a complete fake. "Procrastination is an element in which I live," he wrote. And Daniel Jones said, "Dylan prided himself on preferring the lie to the truth." Nobody, I suppose, will ever know why he didn't turn up to the wedding of the friend who had helped him so much.

He had hurt Vernon so deeply, that, when I first met him in the bar of the Café Royal, there was a shadow between us, and the meeting did little to remove it. Dylan had promised to be waiting in the back bar when we arrived; but he was not there, nor did he arrive until some time later, when Vernon was already beginning to be anxious, but there was a real reason this time. He had been seeing Caitlin and Aeronwy off to Blashford from Waterloo, and had put her luggage, including her handbag with money and tickets, on the wrong train. This had moved off before the mistake had been discovered, and Caitlin had been, naturally, furious. Caitlin in a fury was not an experience to be recommended, and there was a great deal of telephoning, borrowing, soothing down of officials and making of arrangements to be done before she could begin her journey.

Dylan arrived very hot and flustered and only too evidently not at his best. I expected him to ask about the wedding, if not to apologise, and at least to make some enquiry about Vernon's married life; but he seemed wholly preoccupied with his own affairs. He smoked heavily, and clearly intended to drink as much as he could in the shortest time possible. The Café Royal contained several of his friends, who were only too plainly eager to help him in this intention. It was very difficult for me to associate this stout, tobacco-stained imbiber with the poet of *Poem in October* and the other work that Vernon had read to me. I was very young and very censorious, and it has to be said that subsequent meetings with Dylan did not do much to change my first judgment. He was not, in any case, at his best in wartime London; too much and too easy drink, too many and too obsequious admirers, too many drinking clubs open when the pubs were shut, and, for the first time, a salary that he could spend freely. Yes, he was witty and his conversation was brilliant, but only at first; as the drink took over, the talk seemed amusing only to the equally inebriated audience.

I never knew Caitlin in the early, idyllic days of the marriage, nor in its late, violent stages. In these wartime days and after, she was always the incarnation of suppressed rage. In their public quarrels and disagreements, it was always she who spoke in an embittered tone and he who spoke gently, trying to placate and conciliate her. When she was unforgivably rude to a Chinese waiter, Dylan went into the kitchens and, I suppose, apologised to the man and gave him some money. When she audibly grumbled at the badness of a Marx Brothers film (which Dylan and Vernon loved), he first tried to quiet her, and then apologetically left the cinema with her. I never heard him speak to her with anything more than slight irritation; on his side, their quarrels had the harmless quality of a children's squabble, while on her side there was real vindictiveness and a desire to hurt. On the sole occasion that they came to stay with us together, she did not trouble to conceal her boredom and lack of interest in anything to do with our marriage, our house and our child. She did not care for me, and I was always nervous in her presence, which probably brought out the worst in her; but being with her was rather like being in the same room with a tiger which was not very strongly chained.

Dylan's real charm and sincerity, for me at least, showed themselves only in his native Wales. There he was at his best, relaxed and appreciative, not needing to show off, eagerly listening to his friends' talk, laughing hilariously and obviously enjoying his own great enjoyment. I remember him reading the first draft of *August Bank Holiday* to Fred and Mary Janes and Vernon and me, in our small furnished room at the top of Glanmor Hill. (On the mantelpiece there were two metal knights, one holding a candle in his uplifted right hand; the other held one in his left. These caused Dylan the greatest uneasiness. "Could you change them over?" he asked me, and then, a little later, "No, it's no good. Should you mind putting them out of the room? They make my arms ache dreadfully.")

He held the manuscript in his left hand and gestured freely with his right; a glass of beer stood on a table near him, from which he sipped occasionally but did not empty during the half-hour reading. It was the first time I had heard him read, and the effect was mesmerising. The light voice, the subtly comic intonation, the sheer novelty and surprises of the humour, made us listen open-mouthed, and applaud rapturously at the end. "Thanks," he said modestly, "but do you think it's any good *really?*" He always worked hard on both prose and verse, but was quite prepared for other people not to think them as good as he did himself. I once suggested to him, after reading *A Refusal to Mourn* in manuscript, that instead of 'Deep with the first dead lies London's daughter', he might have varied the alliteration by writing, 'Low with the first dead...' I made the suggestion very timidly, but, looking at me with great intensity, he said, "Oh, I do wish I had thought of that." Of course, he had thought of it, and had rejected it, but he never liked to hurt anyone's feelings if he could help it. Of course he did hurt a great many people in his last years, but never, I think, intentionally.

"The war, they say," he wrote to Oscar Williams in March 1945, "is all over bar the dying." On the same day, he wrote to Vernon about an incident in which a Commando captain (subsequently tried for, and acquitted of, attempted murder) fired off a sub-machinegun in the wood-and-asbestos Majoda, Dylan's rented bungalow in Newquay. Although he was terrified, Dylan behaved with great courage, at one point taking the gun away from the enraged man, and only giving it back when threatened with a hand-grenade. "At debt's and death's door I now stand with a revolving stomach, waiting for V1000 and the Bubonic Plague." This incident terrified Vernon too. All his friends, except David Lewis, Wyn's younger brother, had come safely through the war; and in spite of Dylan's continual prophecies of a short life, he saw himself and Dylan growing old like Yeats, their poems 'moving, like Swedenborg's angels, towards the dayspring of their youth'. He wrote to Francis in May,

> I've heard twice lately from Dylan, who was involved in a dangerous incident a month ago... It's a very lucky thing that no life was lost. I loathe fights, and simply don't understand why Dylan has them, but he's very sorry about it all, and says he wasn't provocative at all that evening.

It was in a postscript to the machine-gun letter that Dylan asked Vernon, with great urgency, to write a 'personal introduction' for a book of his selected writings to be brought out in America.

> To me, of course, that introduction coming from you as my friend, and as – we've both said this with a kind of giggling gravity – the only other poet except me whose work I really like today – would be the best in the world. Let me know if you would do it; and if you would, could you do it *terribly* quickly and let me have it so that I can send it off almost at once. It's a lot to ask, and you hardly ever write prose, but… Well, I'll hear from you. We know each other by doing so many things together, from croquet to bathing (me for the first time) in the icy moon, poetry and very high teas, getting drunk, reading, reading, reading, sea staring, Gower, Laugharne, London… I've written thousands of letters to you; if you've kept some you could use what you like to help build up this 'human portrait' of this fat pleader.

An introduction from Vernon might be 'the best in the world' for Dylan, but it did not prevent him from asking other people to have a go. Donald Taylor had been staying at Newquay in March, and Dylan must have asked him to do an introduction, too, because there was a reminder in a letter to Taylor on March 27 (the day before he wrote to Vernon).

> Please don't forget to have a shot at doing those 'personal' thousand words for the introduction to my American Selected Writing. Let me see what you bang out. If you're too busy, I can ask Tommy Earp to do something, but I hope you aren't.

It looks, therefore, as though Dylan was asking several friends to write an introduction, intending to choose the one he thought the most suitable, regardless of the others' waste of time and effort.

If Vernon had known this, I am pretty sure he would have refused. But he did try, and it worried him very much. He sat among the Victorian plush of our landlady's little parlour in Stony Stratford, writing and crossing out and writing and crossing out. "I can't write about my closest friend," he said to me, but he sat up nearly all night, writing the thousand words, and typed them before breakfast so that he could post them in the main post office in Bletchley. "But he won't like it," he said sorrowfully. "I know he won't like it."

Dylan wrote politely:

It was so good of you to write that little personal – what? -thing, then, so quickly and so very nicely. Just, I should imagine, what New Directions want, and I have sent it off *just* as it is, not even altering 'good' to 'great' or putting in a paragraph about my singing voice or horsemanship. Thank you a lot. It did, I know, sound rather awful: Write about me. If you had asked me to do it about you, I should have pleaded everything from writer's cramp to never having met you except in the dark, and then only once.

But Vernon was despondent. "It wasn't what he wanted," he said. "I've let him down. I knew he wouldn't like it." Years afterwards, in a note to the *Letters*, he wrote:

The American edition of *Selected Writings...* did not afterwards use a personal note. I did write one... but I did not, so far as I can remember, quote from any of his letters. Nor was the note at all adequate or satisfactory, for what one is asked to do is never either, unless it is done without embarrassment. My own embarrassment was acute, like that of a man holding a many-coloured kite on a windless day.

Dylan did not return the unused note, and Vernon, in his hurry to post it, had not taken a copy. I was sorry, because it seemed to me both illuminating and amusing, and I cannot understand why it was not used. But Vernon, rightly or wrongly, felt that what he had written had displeased Dylan in some way. He heard nothing of him between April 1945 and May 1946. *Deaths and Entrances* was published in February 1946, and was the first of Dylan's books of which a copy had not been sent to Vernon on publication. He bought about two dozen copies, and sent them to all his friends and relations. "Its poems are wonderful, and the best he has written," he wrote to Francis. "...He's not much of a correspondent – to me, anyway, though he used to be." Again:

> I'm glad you are making good use of your translation of Dylan's *'A Prospect of the Sea.'* He seems to have deserted me now that he is permanently in London but if he does come to Swansea I'll be glad to see him. His book has been very well received and they are certainly the most beautiful lyrical poems he has written. I do not like the very occasional word-tricks, 'once below a time', 'happy as the heart was long', because I do not think they are poetry, or even Dylan Thomas, but Joyce's ghost walking. But they are tiny blemishes in grand and lovely work.

He used to say, after Dylan's death, in talks all over England, Wales and America, that Herbert Read was the sole reviewer to say the only possible thing about the book: "These poems cannot be reviewed; they can only be acclaimed."

Vernon had seen all, and helped with some, of the poems in *Deaths and Entrances,* except *Fern Hill,* and was thus very closely involved with them. Although he held to his view that no poet should ever review the work of another living poet, he lost no opportunity of proclaiming, in lectures and poetry-readings, his belief that these poems were great.

> Out of the dust of bombed London he raised the victims of tragedy to their own dignity and the glory which he, as a religious witness, acclaimed. Such poems are *A Refusal to Mourn the Death, by Fire, of a Child in London* and *Ceremony After a Fire Raid.* In others, like *Fern Hill* and *Poem in October* the praise of life is unfolded, in stanzas of vivid colour and compelling, assonantal music, through a recreation of his own boyhood. He had at first doubts over the stanza form of *Vision and Prayer,* in which the verses of the first part formed the shape of a diamond and the verses of the second part the shape of an hour-glass...The

device was one that George Herbert had used, a poet whom Dylan had particularly loved and admired. Yet the poem had found its original spur in the work of a very different poet. Dylan told me, when he was just beginning to write it, that he had read a most wonderful statement of Rilke about God being born in the next room. This must, I think, have been the poem *Du Nachbar Gott* from the *Stundenbuch*. *Vision and Prayer* was rightly acclaimed as a fine religious poem. I had suggested to him that, although the words of the first part appeared to fit the diamond-pattern organically, there were verses in the second part where the words seemed to have been drilled into position to fit the pattern of the prayer-wheel and the line-endings did not coincide with the pauses of the voice, as they do, for instance, in Herbert's *Easter Wings*. So I wondered whether he would consider trying out the second part in verses with lines of equal length. The suggestion did not appeal to Dylan at all. He had chipped out his poem with consummate care, working on it for months like an old carpenter, and he did not want to change it. He was right to stick to the pattern in which the poem had been conceived, and I do not see now how he could have changed it without writing a different poem.

Vernon made a suggestion about *Poem in October* which met with more success.

He did alter 'bare' to 'winged' trees in the second stanza and 'brown with October blood' (which was my only criticism) to 'leaved with October blood' in the last. It was the most beautiful poem he had made, and one of the most beautiful, I think, in the language.

In a talk which Vernon gave at Attingham Park, he analysed the reasons why he thought *Deaths and Entrances* not only great but unique.

First, there is a particular way in which Dylan uses language to stir the imagination. Word-play and puns are used as a creative element and colloquialisms are made dynamic by their context. Phrases that hit the ear with one meaning are found, on examination, to have a second and deeper meaning. Second, the religious base of his poems is organic and consistent. When asked to describe his poems and what they meant to him Dylan called them 'Statements on the way to the Grave.' Third, the images of birds, creatures, fruit and all living things are seen from the point of view of their Creator, from the Book of Genesis. Fourth, pattern-making and symmetry are a strong element in the structure of these poems. The demands of exact pattern are very seldom neglected.

Vernon had, of course, in spite of Dylan's long silence, written to him about *Deaths and Entrances*, but Dylan did not reply; he had been moving about, until he came to rest in Holywell Ford, in Oxford, in March 1946. By then, Vernon had been demobilised and was back in Wales.

Chapter 10

A SINGLE VOICE

So dear to thought are these remembered things. – V. W.

Vernon's second book, *The Lamp and the Veil*, was published while he was still in uniform, late in 1945. The reviews ranged from *The Listener*'s, "Nothing comparable has been published since *Little Gidding*," to *Time and Tide*'s, "How that Mr Watkins does go on." But from the critic for whom Vernon cared most there came no word, not even a letter of thanks for the book, which had, of course, been sent to him before publication. It was the more disappointing since, in two of the three long poems of which the book consisted, Dylan made a personal appearance. Walter Allen, in *Time and Tide,* not only reviewed *The Lamp and the Veil* with *Deaths and Entrances*, but also quoted the verse from *Yeats in Dublin* in which:

> An image stands on Carmarthen sands
> With the black birds overhead.

Yet he made no connection; not a single critic connected this 'image' and 'the extravagant hero of night' with Dylan Thomas.

To say that Vernon was hurt is to trivialise his feelings. He loved Dylan unconditionally, and, therefore, expected nothing in return; but he had rushed home from Ireland to Laugharne with his first draft of the Yeats poem, and had worked hard on two subsequent versions, with Dylan's help. The other two poems were about their own blitzed Swansea, and the last one, *The Broken Sea*, was dedicated to Francis Dufau-Labeyrie's daughter, Vernon's god-child, born in Paris in 1940. It was, in part, a celebration of the shared past of those three young men:

'All the villainies of the fire-and-brimstone-visited town.'

Everywhere there were small reminders to and of Dylan:

> The world of a child's one town...
> Between Cwmdonkin's railing and black-faced Inkerman Street.

It would have meant a great deal to him to know that Dylan noticed and cared for these things. Perhaps he did, but he did not find time to tell Vernon so. He was no longer living in London, but in Oxford, in 'a converted telephone-kiosk, with a bed where the ledge for directories used to be'; in fact, in a summer-house kindly lent him by Margaret Taylor. In April 1946, the long silence was broken. Dylan wrote,

> There's never been such a long time between our letters, and I hope, atom willing, there won't be again…It's been my fault, of course, that goes without whining.

His reason for writing was to borrow Vernon's essay on Wilfred Owen, since he himself was about to do a programme on Owen for the BBC. He also came to visit us in Glanmor Road, which was very near his childhood playground, Cwmdonkin Park; but, apparently, he had no wish to revisit it. In the bitter winter of 1947, he was again in Swansea, gathering material for *Return Journey*. He and Vernon walked about the snow-covered ruins of their past and reminded each other of places where they had been happy. He must have known then that he had been selected to be one of the readers in the broadcast of Vernon's *Ballad of the Mari Lwyd,* but it was not until Vernon wrote to tell him, two weeks later, about this broadcast that he volunteered this information. Vernon was delighted; and, indeed, Dylan was a superb Leader of the Dead. It is nothing less than tragic that the BBC should have destroyed all recordings of this magnificent performance. Of course, Vernon wrote an ecstatic letter, but no answer came from Dylan.

His next letter did not come until more than a year later, in answer to Vernon's request for permission to use his poem *Among Those Killed in the Dawn Raid Was a Man Aged a Hundred.* It began:

> I'm going to write an enormous letter very soon, to make up

for this long, long but never unthinking silence… And I'll send my new poem too.

But he never did.

In April 1948, more than a year after the *Mari Lwyd* broadcast, Patric Dickinson asked Vernon to compile one of his Time For Verse programmes for the BBC Home Service. These consisted of half-an-hour of poetry, often on a single theme. Vernon chose poems about old age. He was to read the prose commentary, and he asked for Dylan and V. C. Clinton-Baddeley to read the verse. Clinton-Baddeley had a deep, musical voice, and had been trained as a verse-reader by Yeats himself.

Vernon had strong views on the reading of poetry, and especially disliked dramatic reading. He said that actors were usually thinking of themselves, while a verse-reader must think only of the verse he was reading. To his mind, a poem should be read with as much care as a musical score; just as a musician would not dream of ignoring a rest, or play a crotchet as a minim, no more should a verse-reader ignore the end of a line of verse, so that the poem sounded like prose. He was fond of quoting William Morris, who is said to have left a reading of his poems saying morosely, "It took me a damned long time to get that into verse." Both the rhythm and the tempo of a poem should be clearly perceptible to the trained or the intuitive ear. But his greatest condemnation was reserved for those who read poems 'with expression'. He felt that the poet had taken very great trouble to select the words which most exactly conveyed the feeling he wished to present. All the reader had to do was to say the words with the correct rhythm; if he also added emotion, the transmission would be overloaded or confused. This was another reason why he disliked actors reading. They had been trained to a different technique, and could rarely leave the poem alone to do its own work. He set out his own theories in a reading at Stratford-on-Avon in 1958:

> I was asked the other day what advantage it was to hear a poet read his own work. I answered, 'However badly he reads, he has one overwhelming advantage. He heard the poem first.'

My questioner was not satisfied. 'Surely,' he said, 'when a poet has written a poem, his work is done? He can then leave it to someone else, to the best-trained person, to interpret it.' He contended that a poet was a professional writer, but an amateur reader, and that a professional work demanded a professional interpretation. It seems to me that an actor is often too conscious of the audience and too little conscious of the poem. In satirical or dramatic verse an actor may excel, but in lyric poetry everything depends upon the discipline of the poem. No reader of lyric poetry will succeed who does not observe a monotonous base. I am easily misunderstood here. I do not mean, of course, that the whole of any lyric poem must be read on one note. I mean that the intensity of a poem is more likely to be felt and kept if it is held down by the strictness of its pattern. That is why, though I have heard Tennyson splendidly read by different people, I have only once heard the exactness of rhythm which entirely communicated the poem, and that was in an old cylindrical recording of Tennyson reading himself. This brings me to my final point: whatever the duty of an actor is towards an audience, the poet's duty is very clear. He must not do more than reproduce the poem as he heard it at the final moment of composition.

Vernon was speaking here to an audience of teachers of verse-speaking, and many of them profoundly disagreed with him. In an address to the Poetry Society in 1966, he described the follow-up:

> I was thanked in a very kind letter and told that my way of reading, with a little adjustment, could be perfectly adapted to a poetry audience. Then the letter went into more detail, recommending expression and variations of pitch. I replied that I *could* read like that, but only did so when I was imitating… the way in which I hated to hear poetry read aloud.

Dylan and Vernon were pretty well agreed as to the way in which they liked poetry to be read, though Dylan was incomparably the more impressive because of his magnificent voice. They both steadfastly refused invitations to judge verse-speaking competitions, having been warned by Dylan's experience in hearing a verse-speaking choir reciting *And Death Shall Have No Dominion*:

> Oh dear. Picked voices picking the rhythm to bits, chosen elocutionists choosing their own meanings, ten virgins weeping slowly over a quick line, matrons mooing the refrain, a conductor with all his vowels planed to the last e.

But Vernon had one great advantage over Dylan in the reading of verse. Although he played no instrument, he listened constantly to music, and his ear for variations of rhythm was extremely subtle. Dylan, as Dr Daniel Jones has pointed out, was musically illiterate. Rhythm was not an important element of poetry for him.

Dr Jones is, as far as I know, the only critic who has pointed out that Dylan, 'never established in his mind the obvious connection between word-stress and musical accent'. Dylan's verse was based almost entirely on quantitative metre rather than accentual metre. (By quantitative metre I mean a metre in which the same number of syllables occurs in each line. In accentual metre, the stresses on certain syllables in every line conform to an accepted pattern.) Of course, Dylan could write accentual verse, but when he did, how did he hear it? It seems likely that he heard all accentual verse as though it were syllabic. How else can one account for his failure, for it was no less, to read it? I heard him attempt to read it, and fail miserably, several times.

The first time was at the rehearsal of the *Old Age* programme. There was a little embarrassment when the two readers turned up, as they had not been speaking to each other for several months, and neither was aware that the other was to be his co-reader. But they shook hands civilly enough, with apologies and compliments equally insincere, and settled down to rehearse. Vernon began the commentary with an anonymous reference to Dylan:

I once asked a friend if he would go to a party where all the guests were under eighteen, and he refused; but he added that if they had all been over eighty he would have gone.

Clinton-Baddeley read Shakespeare's *Crabbed Age and Youth*, after which Dylan was to read A. E. Housman's *Fancy's Knell*, with its beautiful verse:

> Wenlock Edge was umbered,
> And bright was Abdon Burf,
> And warm between them slumbered
> The smooth green miles of turf;
> Until from grass and clover
> The upshot beam would fade,
> And England over
> Advanced the lofty shade.

In this, the delicate rhythm of the seventh line is entirely dependent on its five syllables being spoken in exactly the same time as the six syllables of all the other lines. Dylan could not see this; worse, he could not read the six-syllable lines as accentual metre at all. The poem was ruined. At first, Vernon tried reading the poem to him correctly, but without success. Then Clinton-Baddeley joined in, and this proved disastrous: from being flushed and petulant, Dylan was on the verge of a real tantrum. He had to read the poem as he wanted; at the suggestion that he should read the Shakespeare and Clinton-Baddeley the Housman, he threatened to walk out. It was clear that he thought the others were ganging up on him, and that he could not see the point they were making. He was still thoroughly ruffled when his turn came to read his own poem, *Among Those Killed In the Dawn Raid Was a Man Aged a Hundred*. He read the first two lines perfectly:

> When the morning was walking over the war
> He put on his clothes and stepped out and he died,

and then disaster struck. He could not manage the first half of the next line:

> The locks yawned loose and a blast blew them wide

He tried, 'the locks lawned loose;' and he tried, 'the yocks yawned loose.' Really desperate now, he hurried over, 'the lawns locked loose,' and 'the yawns loosed locks.' We all watched in fascinated horror as his face grew redder, the veins on his forehead pulsed faster, and the long-awaited tantrum arrived. He jumped up, hurled his book across the rehearsal room and, bawling out, "Oh, God! I'd never have written the bloody line if I'd known it was going to be as hard as this to read!" he made for the door. He was, of course, soothed, comforted and admired; and the live broadcast an hour later went off without a hitch. But the scene was very unlike Dylan, who made slips in verse-reading only when drunk, and not very often then. The virtuoso who could read Dai's Boast from *In Parenthesis* and Hopkins's *The Leaden Echo and the Golden Echo* without a single fluff was not likely to wreck half a line of one of his own poems unless something had happened to upset him. Although it seemed then (and seems now) wildly unlikely that Dylan could not hear accentual metre when read by others, it was only too obvious that he could not reproduce it himself.

I knew then why Dylan, although he was superb as Satan in *Paradise Lost*, yet created a feeling of unease in dialogue. It was because he was reading Milton in syllabic metre, while everybody else in the programme was reading him in accentual metre. It would have been much better if he had read the whole poem himself.

This was not an isolated occasion. Dr Jones has told the story of Dylan's trying and failing to write a poem to be sung to the Londonderry Air. "It was impossible to explain to Dylan why it does not follow that a phrase of music requiring ten syllables can be sung to any ten-syllable line." And Roy Campbell, who handled many of Dylan's Third Programme readings, said that he had difficulty with 'correct' poets like Pope and Dryden. And in another programme with Vernon, the same problem arose. Dylan was reading three of Vernon's sea ballads, and Vernon spoke the prose commentary. They ran into trouble with the second poem, *Ballad of the Three Coins*, which begins:

I know this road like the back of my hand

> From birth to the lonely sea
> With a windblown dog and a bottle of sand,
> And I count my curses three.

Dylan had never heard the idiom 'like the back of my hand', and laid enormous emphasis on the nouns, thus making the line virtual nonsense. Then he wiped the simple, strongly-accented ballad rhythm out of existence by his weighty syllabic reading. But his voice and manner were always magnificent, and the destruction by the BBC of these two programmes seems not only pointless but very short-sighted.

Another programme in which Vernon and Dylan took part, this time with Daniel Jones, Alfred Janes and John Prichard, was broadcast on the Welsh Home Service, and rather pretentiously called *Swansea and the Arts*; but it was not at all pretentious in content. Five artists, three writers, a composer and a painter, all friends, talked about the town and its effect on their work. It is interesting, too, because it is almost the only public expression on record of Dylan's opinion of Vernon.

> First of all, then, Vernon Watkins, poet and present. I think him to be the most profound and greatly accomplished Welshman writing poems in English, and he is one of the few poets I know intensely occupied with his craft, who happily makes a living in a way that has nothing to do with words. So many writers, because their own serious writing does not pay, live by writing about writing, lecturing about writing, reviewing other writers, script-writing, advertising, journalising, boiling pots for the chain store publishers; Vernon Watkins writes nothing but poems. Very properly, he makes his living by other people's money: in a bank. He is proof against the dangers (so tempting to poets, such as myself, who are not qualified to extract their livelihoods other than by the use of language) the dangers of mellifluous periphrasis, otiose solipsism, the too-easy spin and flow of the paid word.

Vernon and Dylan made one television appearance together, in April 1953. The performers also included Alfred Janes and Dr Daniel Jones (not John Prichard as Dr Jones has said). Wynford Vaughan-Thomas acted as a kind of linkman. The scene was supposedly Janes' studio, and his paintings, portraits of Dylan and Vernon, Swansea and Gower led to the 'bits' spoken by each participant. Dylan was not, for some reason, at his ease in this programme, and Vernon admitted that, "Dylan couldn't quite remember his words."

Vernon's third book of poems, *The Lady with the Unicorn*, was published in 1948. If Dylan did not buy it, he at least took the trouble to tell Vernon that he had bought it and left it, *at once*, in a cab:

Before I had opened it... Now I must wait till Christmas to read you.

Of course, Vernon immediately sent him another copy, to which he replied,

Lovely book... I am reading it from the beginning, some every night, slow and light and lifted... I'll write again when I've read all the (to me) new beautiful poems.

But, again of course, he did not; though once none of Vernon's poems would have been new to him. Although Dylan was to live another five years, this was the last letter Vernon was ever to receive from him, with the exception of a short note after Vernon had written to him on the death of his father.

Although there were no more letters, there were, in the last years of Dylan's life, a few meetings. When he was in Swansea, Dylan would drop into the Bank in St. Helen's Road, and he and Vernon would have lunch together, or would go to a cricket-match to see Glamorgan play. It was at one such county match that Dylan first told Vernon and Dan about the new piece he was writing which, provisionally called *The Village That Was Mad*, later turned into *Under Milk Wood*. In its very early days, this was to be an account of a village that was so wicked by chapel standards that it was to be tried by a jury consisting of delegates from other Welsh villages. As each of the villagers confessed his sins, the jury would roar, "*Ych-y-fi!*" in appreciative condemnation. It later turned out that the BBC would, in no circumstances, finance a male voice choir for this purpose.

Before the beginning of the end, there was one meeting that brought some of the old friends together again, and gave them, for the space of an afternoon and evening, an unalloyed happiness.

Chapter 11

'ONE DAY
OF THE GREAT LOST DAYS'

Park-Keeper: I think he was happy all the time. – D. T.

One Saturday afternoon in June 1950, Alfred Janes and his wife Mary brought Dylan and Caitlin to Pennard, to spend the rest of the day at The Garth. Dan Jones and his wife and son, Ethel Ross and Elizabeth Iorwerth Jones were to come later. It was, I should think, the last time such a group of old Swansea friends was together. Elizabeth was one of the founder members of the Swansea Little Theatre. She had first become aware of Dylan when she was on stage ("I expect I was giving my all," she said) when she heard a member of the audience being, or pretending to be, realistically sick. A chair was overturned, and someone rushed out, making vomiting noises all the time. "It was that *awful* Dylan Thomas," said Eileen Llewellyn Jones, the principal producer, who had had a lot of trouble with Dylan and rehearsals. This incident may have contributed to his being asked to leave the Little Theatre. During the war, Elisabeth and Dylan were scheduled to broadcast a poetry programme together, in Llanelli, since the Swansea studio was considered too dangerous. She was naturally apprehensive; but Dylan was waiting in the studio when she arrived, read and behaved perfectly, and invited her to tea at a small teashop afterwards, and was, she said, "absolutely charming."

It was a fresh, sunny day, and Caitlin and Vernon were eager to bathe. We all started off along the cliffs, to go down to Pobbles Bay, the children romping and squealing ahead of us, but we had hardly gone to the next headland, when Dylan threw himself down on the grass, panting. "I can't possibly walk any further," he said. "I'll wait here till you come up." The others were determined to have their swim, so I politely turned back with Dylan. We sat on the lawn in the shade, he sipping at a glass of lager, and talking agreeably. It was the first time I had felt really at ease with him.

(When the others came back from the bay, I was so exhilarated by our conversation that I rushed indoors and scribbled some notes – sort of paragraph headings – on a pad by the telephone, which I then thought no more about. When I was moving house three years ago, and scrabbling through a bundle of old files and papers, I found this pad. So I am able to construct our talk, not in exact words, of course, but what follows is roughly the order of conversation.)

G W: Caitlin told me once that you read a great deal of Dickens. (*What she actually said was, "Dylan reads Dickens all the bloody time when he ought to be working."*)

D W: I *love* Dickens. I could read him all day, end to end, and then begin again.

G W: What is your favourite book?

D W: How can anybody say that? *David Copperfield, Little Dorrit, Our Mutual Friend,* – well, probably *Bleak House.* I love all the bits about the Ghost's Walk. But I like the earlier ones too. Mr Pecksniff is wonderful.

G W: Yes; and don't you love Newman Noggs? Where he is asked if the new Kenwigs baby is a nice one, and after a bit he says, 'It ain't a very nasty one.'

D W: That's glorious, and so is Mrs. Kenwigs ironing the little girls' pigtails. *And* Mrs. Gamp and Betsy Prig, where she questions the existence of Mrs. Harris! (*Laughs consumedly*)

G W: *My* favourite bit of Mrs. Gamp is when she says about her children, 'My own... has fallen out of three-pair backs, and had damp doorsteps settled on their lungs, and one was turned up smiling in a bedstead unbeknown.'

D W: (*Laughs and chuckles till he is almost breathless, and spills some beer*) Wonderful! What an imagination! to be able to write like that!

G W: I think you do write like that sometimes.

D W: 'Praise to the face is open disgrace,' one of my uncles used to say, sanctimonious bastard. (*Pause while he drinks*) I could never write like Dickens; nobody could.

G W: Well, *Return Journey* is based on the same idea as *Master B.'s Room* in *The Haunted House*. (*Runs into the house and brings back books*) You know, the man tracing his own life back to his boyhood and childhood. (*Finds place in book; reads*) No other ghost has haunted the boy's room...than the ghost of my own childhood, the ghost of my own innocence, the ghost of my own airy belief. Many a time have I pursued the phantom – never with this man's stride of mine to come up with it, never with these man's hands of mine to touch it, never more to this man's heart of mine to hold it in its purity. That is very much the way you look at childhood, in some of your poems and in the ending of *Return Journey*; you know, where the Narrator says, 'What has become of him now?' and Park-keeper says, 'Dead... Dead... Dead... Dead.'

D W: (*Takes the book, and begins to turn the pages, occasionally stopping to read bits*)

G W: (*After a silence.*) There is something I have always wanted to ask you. Do you remember one day, when you first knew Vernon, his mother asked you and Wyn Lewis and Fred to tea? And after tea, because none of you were married, she asked what quality you would look for first in a wife. Wyn Lewis said, 'Sensuality,' which shocked her dreadfully; but you said, 'Seriousness.' (*A pause, while G. W. takes her courage in both hands*) Well, that surprised me, because you don't always behave as though you were a very serious person.

D W: (*Scornfully*) Oh, *behaviour...* I am fundamentally a very serious person. If you want to write the kind of poems I want to write, you must be serious. Otherwise, you write rubbish.

This is substantially the only long conversation I ever had with Dylan. Besides the notes, I have a very good memory for words, and can turn today to the small book which contains Dickens' Christmas stories from *All the Year Round,* with the marvellous *Mrs. Lirriper's Lodgings, Somebody's Luggage, The Haunted House* and all the other works of Dickens's late genius. When I look at the bits which Dylan read out as he leafed through its pages, I can hear his whole-hearted, open-mouthed laughter – a laugh like that of a child, rather high-pitched, ending in a giggle. It was the first time I had heard him laugh like that, with such enjoyment. He laughed a great deal during that afternoon with his old Swansea friends. I was never to hear him laugh after that day was ended.

When Vernon came back from the bay with the children, Caitlin was not with him; she had stayed to have another swim. Only when bathing or dancing (but I never saw her dance) did she seem to throw off the bitterness that by this time pervaded her whole personality. There were plenty of reasons for this: she never had a home of her own, and was forced to drag her children from rented rooms to relatives' grudging help. She never had enough money, and was often left alone with young children while Dylan was living it up in London or America. Sea, scenery and solitude would have been heaven for Vernon; but Dylan, as he explained in his first letter, was a town boy. Laugharne was good for his poems, but not for his leisure; he really needed at intervals the stimulation of pubs and clubs. This was no comfort to Caitlin, though, and by the time Colm was born, she had become a simmering cauldron of rage – by no means always simmering, but often erupting with great violence. But today, she was relaxed from sun and sea, and except for some fairly amiable bickering with Dylan, she sunbathed and talked to Irene, Dan's wife, and the gentle Mary Janes.

As soon as Dan arrived, he and Dylan reverted to their boyhood, as Caitlin said they always did. They began immediately to wrestle, rolling over and over on the grass, struggling and giggling helplessly. Afterwards, they began to act, since both of them loved posturing and making dramatic gestures. All the men there had been to the Uplands Cinema, as children, to the Saturday morning children's programmes, which consisted of comedies and horror movies. What Dylan and Dan now presented was a pastiche of *The Mummy's Claw*, a film at which all four had shuddered as infants. Dan was a mummified Pharaoh, looking noble and aloof, in an old zinc bath standing on end; Dylan an Egyptologist searching tombs, and Vernon a sheepish tomb-robber. (Fred had been ordered to take part, but stood grimly aside, with the expression of suspended criticism he always wore when he thought Dan and Dylan were behaving foolishly.) But although Vernon was no actor at the best of times, he could never refuse Dylan, and wandered through his part with uncertain smiles, frequently being turned round or shoved into place by the impatient hands of the other players.

At tea-time, we all sat on the grass eating sewin sandwiches, *bara brith*, chocolate cake and sponge cake. Dylan asked for pickles, and Caitlin said sharply that his taste buds had been completely destroyed in America through drinking whisky, and that he could taste nothing but salty crisps and vinegar. I brought Dylan a jar of pickle and another of pickled onions.

"Not dead but sleeping," he said, slathering Pan Yan on his sandwich (to gasps of horror from some of the party, since sewin has the most delicate taste of any fish). He kept the jar of onions by him, and sometimes ate one. After tea, Caitlin went for another swim, while Dan swung Dylan on the stout old swing, and Dylan squealed at every downward rush. There was some talk, some playing French cricket with the children, and 'then came still evening on.' The long afternoon was over. It was the last time I saw Dylan.

Vernon saw him on a few occasions after that. He could have gone down to Laugharne, as he used to, but his own life had become very busy, and he may have been made uneasy by the now continual quarrels between Dylan and Caitlin, which he could no longer pretend were not serious. Caitlin now seemed permanently embittered by the circumstances of her life. She made me uneasy and often indignant by her public behaviour, but her life did seem to me intolerable. I suppose the poet's wife has seldom had a bed of roses to lie on, and I thought my life hard enough; but I had at least a permanent roof over my head (though the walls under it were only wood and asbestos), and a regular, if small, income. And Laugharne seemed to me like the end of the world, it was so mournfully lovely and half-dead. Vernon did, however, go to Laugharne once more, when, in the summer of 1953, Francis Dufau-Labeyrie came to Wales. In 1946, his translation of Dylan's *A Prospect of the Sea*, called *Perspective Sur la Mer*, was published in *L'Arche*. After Dylan's death, he wrote to me about this translation, and about Dylan's collected works published by *SEUIL* in 1970:

> I think I should mention that, at the beginning of Vol. ll, they printed a very poor and pedestrian translation of *A Prospect of the Sea*. Apparently they were unaware that *L'Arche* had published my *Perspective Sur la Mer* back in 1946 and their *Une Vue sur la Mer*...carries nothing of the inner movement, enigmatic and from deep below that pervades the original... for which I had the priceless benefit of Vernon's and Dylan's own guidance.

In 1947, *Les Editions de Minuit* brought out *Portrait de l'Artiste en Jeune Chien* (for which there can have been no better translator than Francis, who knew Dylan, Swansea and the Welsh so intimately). He had, in fact, sent Dylan the typescript of his translation before publication, but had no reply. He wrote to Vernon in December 1946:

> I am glad Dylan and Caitlin stayed with you. I have given up every hope of ever getting a letter from him, even a letter of abuse when he sees all the irrelevances of my translation! I take down the address you give me anyway, although I suppose it must be as transient in character as the ones I previously had.

The visit to Laugharne in July 1953, three months before Dylan was to make his last, fatal, visit to America, was in the nature of a reunion, and

Dylan Jones, Alfred Janes, Daniel Jones and Dylan Thomas at the Garth, Pennard, June 1950

Dylan felt it to be so. Francis remembered him coming out of the Boat House to greet them, saying over and over again, as though he could not believe it, "Fifteen years! Fifteen years!" They were all happy, going to Brown's Hotel for drinks, back to the Boat House for lunch, looking out from the balcony over the estuary and Sir John's Hill. Dylan asked about the reception of *Portrait de l'Artiste en Jeune Chien*, and was amused when Francis solemnly repeated the words of the critic Georges Lamerichs; "*Ce fut un succes d'estime.*"

Soon, the tensions, never long absent from that house, showed themselves. Francis asked Dylan to read some poetry, and Dylan (perhaps hoping to propitiate Caitlin) read one of her poems beautifully, and it was much admired. Then, at Vernon's request, he read *Over Sir John's Hill*, giving it, Vernon told me, an inexpressibly moving elegiac tone, his beautiful voice softer than usual, especially at the lines:

> We grieve as the blithe birds, never again, leave shingle and elm,
> The heron and I,
> I young Aesop fabling to the near night...

(I am convinced that the Muse knows when the death of one of her sons is approaching though the poet himself may not know. There are unpublished poems of Vernon's which show a consciousness of approaching death, though he was sure that he would live into old age.) But suddenly, horrifyingly, the tensions erupted. When Dylan read the lines of the last verse:

> ...I see the tilting whispering
> Heron, mirrored, go,
> As the snapt feathers snow,
> Fishing in the tear of the Towy...

he pronounced the word as 'tare'. Caitlin abruptly said it as 'tier'. Dylan became – with some reason – furious. They screamed their own versions of the word back and forth, until Dylan, his face congested, bawled, "But, for Christ's sake, the bloody word is *there* – I wrote it!" He seemed about to attack Caitlin; Colm screamed, and both combatants became sullen and resentful, not speaking to each other. Vernon and Francis were shaken and embarrassed, and went out for a walk. Vernon knew better than to intervene, but the incident remained in his memory, and he referred to it obliquely in his paper on *Eight Poems by Dylan Thomas:*

> Some have suggested that in the line from the nursery rhyme, 'dilly dilly,' Dylan was punning on his own name. That is possible. But it is utterly wrong to read 'Fishing in the tear of the Towy' in the last stanza as 'Fishing in the *tear* of the Towy. I once heard that mistake made by an actor on the wireless. How, I wonder, did he reconcile this to 'the tune of the slow, Wear-willow river', at the end of that last stanza?

(But Dr Hugh Price, a founder and committee member of the Dylan Thomas Society, told me that there exists a recording in which Dylan does pronounce 'tear' as 'tier'. I have not been able to identify it.)

When Vernon and Francis returned after their stroll, Dylan was in his work-shed at the top of the garden. They talked about *Under Milk Wood*, which Dylan was still working on. He said that, although it had been read successfully on stage, he was not yet satisfied with every detail for print. Vernon praised the device in *Over Sir John's Hill* of assonantal rhymes, such as heron, hedges, headstone; dilly, dingle, distant. "Only you would have noticed that," Dylan said, amused. Then, for a little while, they talked about the techniques of poetry, as they used to do in Cwmdonkin Drive and Heatherslade. When it was time to leave, Francis took Dylan's hands in his, and said earnestly, "*Au revoir.*" But Dylan only smiled and waved them goodbye.

Vernon and Dylan met once more, for a short time, when Dylan was in Swansea, on his way to London for his flight to the USA. Dylan described the libretto of the opera he planned to write to Stravinsky's music:

> The opera was to describe the holiness of Earth which had been devastated, leaving alive only one old man and his children. Visitors from another planet would come to take the children away, and the old man, who alone remembered the beauty

and mystery of Earth, would try to describe them to the visitors and to his children, who had been too young to know these things.

(This seems to me more like the plan for a long poem than an opera; there would have to be a good deal more action for a stage setting. Dylan was, in any case, completely unmusical; the songs he liked were those with some kind of word-play, such as Noel Coward's *The Stately Homes of England* or Groucho Marx's *Lydia O Lydia, my Encyclopiddyer*, or some of Cole Porter's lyrics. I do not think he and Stravinsky would have been able to produce anything like an opera.)

Then, once more, Dylan and Vernon were talking about poetry – for the last time, though neither of them knew it.

Dylan told me that the first line of *In the White Giant's Thigh* had taken him three weeks to get right, and for the *Prologue* to the *Collected Poems*, which was the last poem he finished, he used over a hundred and sixty pages of manuscript. No work in the world was harder than the making of a poem, he said.

They talked, too, about how Dylan had held his father's hand as he died, and he quoted the first lines of his unfinished Elegy for his father (which Vernon was later to complete):

> Too proud to die, broken and blind he died
> The darkest way, and did not turn away,
> A cold kind man brave in his narrow pride.

After that, it was time for Vernon to go. Dylan walked a little way towards the bank with him, telling him that Goronwy Rees, then principal of University College, Aberystwyth, wanted to give them both honorary degrees.

"I told him yes for both of us," Dylan said, chuckling. "I said you must be a Doctor of Law and I am going to be a Doctor of Divinity."

They parted, both laughing. Some biographers have thought that Dylan died written out, as it were, with no more poems left in him. Vernon certainly would have disagreed with that view. In that last

Caitlin, Daniel Jones, and Alfred Janes in 'The Mummy's Claw'. Pennard, June 1950

meeting, Dylan seemed to him to be full of fresh and inventive ideas, and to be as passionately committed to poetry as he had ever been.

Yet, since his death, it is most difficult to write of Dylan Thomas with detachment, just as it was most difficult to think of him with detachment when he was alive. He had the faculty of immediacy, of making everything present, and of becoming a part of people's lives almost before he knew them; how much more did he do this when he knew them well. When he went on a journey, theatrical stories about him, each one funnier than the last, began to accumulate; when he returned, all that theatrical scenery, all those props, disappeared, and it was he, in his intense and essentially calm awareness, who discarded them. He was the serious survivor of all his myths. This is now more difficult to understand; for the man who, just before leaving for America for the last time, recited to me the first lines of his unfinished *Elegy* for his father, and the man who, eighteen years earlier, had, in his house above Swansea bay, opened a file and read his poetry to me for the first time, are inextricably bound in a personality from which time has fallen. The slight figure of the boy of twenty who read the first poems and the full figure of the mature, but equally shy, poet who recited the beginning of the *Elegy* speak to me with a single voice.

Chapter 12

PARADOXES

Such darkness lives there, where a last grief sings. – V. W.

Although Vernon did not go to America until 1964, he had American connections and American friends. Constantine FitzGibbon, Dylan's future biographer, had been at Bletchley Park, and so had Robert Hivnor, a writer who lived in New York, and, like Francis Dufau-Labeyrie, corresponded frequently with Vernon. Besides this, Vernon's first book, *Selected Poems*, to be brought out in America, was published in 1947 by New Directions. James Laughlin was the head of this firm, known in the USA, as Faber's was in Britain, as publishers of the best poetry. Laughlin was very tall; I asked Dylan if he had found him pleasant. "Oh, *very* delightful," he said, enunciating every consonant with extreme bitterness. "I was always having conversations with his navel, asking it to lend me money, and it never would."

But New Directions took on the arduous task of selling Dylan's work in the forties, when he was completely unknown in America, and did a very good job. Laughlin wrote to Vernon in 1946:

> It is frightfully hard to get our public here interested in an English poet... Dylan's first two books flopped even though they had good reviews. People here had Auden and Spender in their minds, and these were *the* English poets, and that was that. Now finally Dylan is being recognised here. There have been a good many articles in the little magazines about him, and he has also gotten some good publicity from the attacks of people like the Society for the Preservation of Sanity in Poetry. He is

now their Number One target. We sold 1800 of Dylan's *New Poems* and we are printing 4000 of his *Selected Writings* (which includes D & E) and I think we will sell them.

When Dylan made his first visit to America, in 1950, Vernon was not greatly in favour of it. He recognised the need to make money, of course, but he knew that poems could be created only in solitude and silence, and he grudged the time that would be lost in travelling and social life. Later, when stories filtered back about Dylan's reckless behaviour, he began to feel anxious; he was, anyway, always happier when Dylan was in Wales. Still, he knew the value of Dylan's poetry readings, and was glad that his stature as poet and reader should be recognised. He wrote to all his American friends before the first tour. Bob Hivnor wrote back:

"Do you know any Dylan Thomas stories?" seems to have become a common question where the benighted literary people around here – and I suppose all over America – gather. It seems there are many and since they split up into new stories like a cell dividing soon there will probably be many more.

A few: At a party in his honour at Harvard (or Princeton? or Williams? or Connecticut Women's?) Peter Viereck, an interesting poet and a Professor of History, brought several of his books as gifts to Thomas.

"Here is my book, *Terror and Decorum*."

Thomas: "Ahh." Complete indifference.

"Here is my book, so-and-so."

"Ohh." More indifference.

"And here is my latest book, *Conservatism Revisited*."

"Better it should never have been visited at all."

He was asked by an old lady about political prospects in England and he replies, "All I'm interested in is *breasts!*"

To a comely co-ed at Radcliffe (or Vassar or Smith) he says "Oh, to be suckled at those breasts!"

At one point, he claims to be the only male British poet.

Professor So-and-so says to him at a railroad station, "I am Professor So-and-so of the welcoming Committee, come here to welcome you."

Thomas, goggle-eyed and belching on strange beers, "I'm glad you're Professor So-and-so. I'm glad there's a welcoming committee. I'm glad you're here. I'm glad."

It seems your fellow-citizen is enjoying himself and enacting perfectly the academic American's idea of a poet being irresponsible, undependable, drunk, sexy – at least in word. I heard him recite once and his performance was very good – but a little on the romantic side both in delivery and in poems chosen. He read quite a few Welsh poets on the night I heard him. There was an encore and the chairman asked if anyone in the audience had a request. Many were shouted up and finally one was chosen and a British accent piped up from the back, "Could you choose one a little shorter, please?" I saw him afterward surrounded by women one or two feet taller and got a glimpse of his fine head and face.

Vernon wrote back, encouraging Hivnor to introduce himself to Dylan. They did not, in fact meet, but Hivnor sent a newspaper cutting, which referred to Dylan's saying at one reading that Vernon was the best poet writing in English. Oscar Williams, the poet and anthologist, who had helped Dylan by placing his poems in American periodicals, also wrote to Vernon in March 1950:

We have been seeing a great deal of Dylan here. His readings are magnificent, and all America is in love with him. Unfortunately our distances are fantastic, and Dylan is having something of an ordeal in travelling from our east coast to west coast, stopping off at innumerable places in between. But all the adulation he is receiving doesn't prevent him from being homesick for Wales.

On subsequent trips, too, Vernon tried to keep track of Dylan's movements by writing to friends, but he never wrote to Dylan, or Dylan to him. A few days after Dylan had landed from the SS *United States* to begin his third American tour in April 1953, Vernon wrote to Francis:

> I wish now that I had given Dylan your Montreal address when I saw him a few weeks ago. He is now in America and I don't know his address. Do look out for any notice of his lectures or readings in Montreal. I know he went there on an earlier tour, but this is only a 6 weeks' tour. I don't know whether it will cover Canada as well as the United States. Surely you'll read about it if you take a literary paper. Try to see him.

"…A bulging Apple among poets…"
Sent to Vernon Watkins by Dylan during his first visit to New York in 1950.
An enlargement of a street photograph with the graffiti on it!

About the final tour in mid-September 1953 he had some reason to be anxious. Dylan had told him, when he and Francis visited Laugharne a few weeks before, that he had been having 'black-outs' quite frequently, and that he could no longer eat with comfort or enjoyment, and had sent away to a newspaper for an advertised diet-sheet. (This was from the *Sunday Pictorial,* and turned up among Dylan's effects that came back to Wales after his death). Vernon was disturbed by the mention of the diet-sheet. He had been accustomed, ever since he had first met Dylan, to hear him complain of his asthma, his bronchitis, his gout, his gastritis – even, in the early days, of his tuberculosis; but that Dylan should actually take some action about his health was unheard of. At Laugharne, too, there had been, if not an elegiac, at least a summing-up note, when Dylan talked about his work. "I know I'm good," he had said. "I think I have written a lot of good poetry, but I don't think I've written great poetry. Mozart was both good and great." It sounded as though he were assessing a completed *oeuvre.* John Malcolm Brinnin, meeting Dylan in the same month, felt that, "He wanted above all to come back to America, and that he *would* come back to America." Vernon felt otherwise:

Dylan Thomas spoke of his last tour as a necessity. It was the only one he approached with reluctance. Yet he did look forward, when the period of intensive work in New York would be over, to working with Stravinsky. His intention was to complete the script of *Under Milk Wood,* on which he continued to make revisions, and to handle the performance in New York; and then to go on to Hollywood where he would work on their projected opera. He was, when he left England, in the position of a man who had several difficult hurdles to negotiate before reaching his objective. Had he been well, he would have done this easily. As it was, he hoped that the short blackouts he had occasionally suffered during the previous months would not recur. The project of the opera filled him with enthusiasm. He had sketched out a plan of the libretto in his mind, and he had the greatest regard for Stravinsky.

He knew that he ought to see a doctor, but he feared that the doctor would pronounce him unfit and cancel the trip.

Nevertheless, in spite of foreboding and anxiety, it was with a shock that, on the Thursday before Dylan's death, he saw a headline in a newspaper (shown him by a customer in the bank) saying that Dylan Thomas was lying ill in a New York hospital. This first announcement said nothing about Dylan's being in a coma; and Vernon, though apprehensive, certainly feared nothing more at that time than a major illness for his friend. But the next day's bulletin was more serious, and on Saturday, as soon as the bank closed, he climbed up Constitution Hill to see Dan Jones. Dr Jones, in his book, *My Friend Dylan Thomas*, gives his own account of the telephone calls that were made, and of the comfortless reply that came over the Atlantic. They both knew that Dylan's life was in the balance.

That one scale was descending was proved by a telephone call from the *Times* on Sunday morning, asking whether Vernon would be prepared to write an obituary for Dylan Thomas. At first, he refused, crying, "But he's not dead yet!" He allowed himself to be persuaded, feeling, as he told me, that he, at least, would ignore the myth of the Byronic wastrel, and present a true picture of the man and the poet he knew. He worked for most of Sunday, making and discarding drafts, and at last he read it to me. "This is the only thing I have ever written that I hope will never be published," he said.

All that day, Dylan lay unconscious in New York; Caitlin was dragged from his bedside to a psychiatric clinic on Long Island; and Vernon typed and discarded with a heavy heart. On the same day, in a house in Chelsea, Ceri Richards had been reading Dylan's *Collected Poems,* and illustrating some of them. He paused in this occupation to write to Vernon:

> Frances and I are very distressed over the dangerous news of Dylan – it appears to be really very critical – we only hope that by some miracle he will survive and come back to Wales very soon. It is a great pity he has to make these jaunts to the USA,

although of course it is a great occasion to be working with
Stravinsky. I have been reading from his Collected Works this
weekend and his trouble deepens the tragedy in the poems
– also, while reading in his book, I have decorated many of the
pages – if Dylan gets well soon (we hope so, so very much) then
I think of sending him a copy complete with the drawings.

Ceri Richards had left Swansea to live in London, but spent most of
his holidays in Pennard, where he had bought a small bungalow. In 1945,
he had been commissioned by Tambimuttu, the editor of *Poetry (London)*
to illustrate *The Force That Through the Green Fuse Drives the Flower*. To
respond to Dylan's poems was a sure way to Vernon's heart, and he and
Ceri became close friends. Ceri drew and painted illustrations of Vernon's
poems, Vernon wrote poems and articles about Ceri's paintings. They
responded with love and sensitivity to each other's work, because their
views of life were so similar – they understood each other intuitively.
They looked on nature and humanity from the same viewpoint, both
saw creation as praise, and both were aware of the intensity that was
needed to create a work of art. Vernon talked a great deal about Dylan to
Ceri, and they made many plans to meet him, but somehow these plans
were never successful. Then, the day before Dylan left for his final tour,
Alfred Janes drove Ceri down to Laugharne. Ceri described the meeting
in a letter to Vernon:

> I am truly thankful for the opportunity Fred and Mary gave
> me to meet him – and to meet him at Laugharne – I liked him
> at once – I felt a shyness, for I was a stranger and come with
> some curiosity even though it was with warmth and admiration
> – and Fred and Mary were very old companions – I think we
> would have come to like one another very much and I would
> love to have had other meetings with him – but as you say
> Vernon – if I had missed him then, I would have been filled
> with regret.
>
> I am very happy to have met Caitlin with Dylan – I am

afraid there was a great sadness in Caitlin that day for she was worried at Dylan's departure. What a profound pity she didn't go with him at last.

The Boat House home was a melancholy but very beautiful place – and according to Dylan he never saw many people – well, it was rather remote – but he filled it with his resounding voice and friendliness, and Swansea too.

It was important to Vernon that two people who meant so much to him should have met each other. When Dr Daniel Jones comments on the 'crazy irrelevance' of such a remark, on hearing of Dylan's death, as, "What a good thing he just managed to meet Ceri Richards," he misunderstands Vernon's feelings. In fact, this meeting was to have a great effect on Ceri, and on the drawings, lithographs and paintings that he was to create in Dylan's memory. On hearing of Dylan's death he wrote:

> Since his illness I have read his work with much greater understanding for his tragedy sings more clearly in his work it seems:
>
> > O, let me midlife mourn by the shrined
> > And druid heron's vows
> > The voyage to ruin I must run...
> > Yet, though I cry with tumbledown tongue,
> > Count my blessings aloud:
> > And right to the end.
>
> ...no-one has read him with more love than I – or your work – and to work for visual equivalents in response to your poems – I have tried to meet imagery with imagery and meaning with meaning.

On that Sunday in October, no love or thoughts of his friends could hold Dylan back from the silences of eternal night. He was slipping away; and on Monday at midday he died. Vernon's obituary appeared in the *Times* on Tuesday. It resembled other *Times* obituaries only in that it was anonymous. It bothered hardly at all with the biographical details that are usually the substance of obituaries: it concentrated almost entirely on Dylan's stature as a poet, writer and broadcaster, and on the true persona under the many masks.

He approached the great masters of his art with an impudent suspicion, because from the first he distrusted the academic approach. Yet, when they had walked with him through the furnace of his own imagination and emerged unscathed, there was no man who loved them more. Indeed, no poet of the English language has so hoodwinked and confuted his critics. None has ever worn more brilliantly the mask of anarchy to conceal the true face of tradition. There was nothing God ever made that Dylan Thomas, the revolutionary, wanted to alter. The careful compounder of explosive imagery believed only in calm.

Yet there was nothing topical in his work. The most mistaken of its admirers were those who loved it for its novelty. It was, even in its first phases, an ancient poetry, not rejecting antiquity for the present but seeking, with every device of language, the ancestry of the moment.

It is likely that by his death the world has lost a masterpiece. What it has not lost is the work of a poet who was able to live Christianity in a public way, and whose work distilled it – a poet narrow and severe with himself and wide and forgiving in his affections. Innocence is always a paradox, and Dylan Thomas presents, in retrospect, the greatest paradox of our time.

Other papers might print accounts of Dylan's riotous life; here it was ignored, not for prudish or prudential reasons, but because it was essentially of no importance. It was acclaimed as a tour-de-force, and has been continually reprinted. John Berryman's reaction is typical of many:

I must thank you with all my heart for writing the *Times* obituary. I don't see how you did it. Sickened by the one in the

NY Times I went up to Times Square next day to get the *Times*, which I read with astonishment and respect. I am with you absolutely as to the special importance of *Deaths and Entrances*, and I am glad you went so far. He was one of the greatest poets who ever lived. I want the piece known in this country and showed it last night to the editor of *New World Writing...* and *Partisan Review* will print it if you and the *Times* will allow it.

When it was reprinted, the reaction of reviewers was the same. The *New York Times Book Review* of an anthology said:

> ... there's no better or more definitive item in the book than the unsigned but justly celebrated obituary of Dylan Thomas which first appeared in *The London Times*.

Dylan's death was a crushing blow to Vernon, but, for the moment, he had no time to feel its full weight. Dylan had died intestate, and Caitlin and the three children were destitute. A fund was started in New York to pay Dylan's hospital and mortician's fees, and the expenses for bringing the body back, but it was clear that some long-term provision for the family must be made. Other fund-raising activities were soon put in motion. Dr Daniel Jones, Alfred Janes, Vernon and two other friends of Dylan's called on the Mayor of Swansea and read him a letter from the sponsors of the American fund – W. H. Auden, E. E. Cummings, Marianne Moore, Arthur Miller, Wallace Stevens and Tennessee Williams – which resulted in the opening of the Mayor's Fund.

Reporters telephoned, letters arrived, and there was a rapidly organised radio tribute to Dylan, on the day after his death, of which Vernon wrote to Francis:

> I would have written before but all the time has been caught up in telephone calls. I was with Dan Jones on Saturday and he cabled twice and phoned the New York hospital. Everything that could be done for Dylan was done but the tragedy is that it was not enough to save him.
>
> I read poems of his and Dan spoke a short tribute and played

one of his own short piano compositions in a wireless tribute
to him on Tuesday.

My dear Francis, how glad I am that you saw him again on
that happy and beautiful day before he died. He told me that he
found you 'just the same,' and the reunion was good.

Mrs Thomas is wonderfully brave. I have rung Brown's
(opposite) several times, and they say she is bearing the news
wonderfully.

Vernon's natural desolation was increased by the rumours, accusations,
innuendoes and denunciations that burst out as soon as Dylan died. He
wanted very much to know what had really happened. Fortunately, Bob
Hivnor, who wrote from New York as soon as he heard the news, gave
him the address of John Berryman, the one person who was at Dylan's
bedside at the moment of his death. Vernon wrote to him at once, and
received an immediate answer:

Of course I understand there is no question of curiosity in your
asking. My god! I will tell you as much as I can in a letter. But
the dreadful truth is that I have nothing to tell you that will not
grieve you. I suppose it is better to be grieved by facts than by
mysteries. It is certainly the most terrible thing that has ever
happened in my experience. I can't expurgate it either, writing
to you as Dylan's friend, though of course you will when you
pass any of it on, or perhaps you will feel as I do, that the truth
is what matters. If I don't put it well, forgive me; my brains are
broken.

He had been working too hard at rehearsals, was depressed
and of course drinking. He was talking about the Garden
of Eden. The last time I saw him conscious (not very) was
Saturday, at Harvey Breit's; he was loaded, and hardly able to
speak, though we had some talk about Ted Roethke's drinking.
Monday afternoon he told someone that he had never been
so drunk in his life as Sunday when he went through three
parties.

Wednesday night he was having mild D.T.s in his room here in the Chelsea, and went into coma. Apparently now, at this moment, his mind died. Two friends, who were with him, got him into Emergency at St. Vincent's, and half a dozen people worked on him all Thursday. But after they got his organs into working order, there was really nothing they could do except maintain breathing and nutrition, keep him clear of mucus and administer anti-convulsants; it was up to him. He was in continuous crisis for four and a half days until he died at about twenty minutes to one, Monday afternoon. He was never conscious for a moment and had no pain. One of his best doctors told me immediately after his death that there had never been the slightest hope; but of course we did not know that. They thought there was water on the brain… but they couldn't even be sure of that. His condition was so extreme throughout that all they could exclude was haemorrhage: a spinal tap showed there was none. Under prolonged coma of this sort, the likelihood of severe brain damage is so great that it ought to be impossible to be sorry he did not survive. By a piece of the worst luck in the world (Caitlin was hysterical, she smasht an image and tried to strangle John Brinnin and had to be put in restraint, and everyone else at the hospital was downstairs), I was the only one there when he died. His body died utterly quiet, and he looked so tired that you might once more have burst into tears too, but your grief would have been general, for the whole catastrophe not for the moment. I wish I could say something to help your feelings. It is a fraction of something, I think, that he did not have to die, as some other great poets have had to die, under the impression that what they had done was not worth doing. But this will not help you much. It doesn't help me.

Vernon showed this letter, I believe, to no-one but Ceri Richards and myself. Berryman's description of the quiet, tired body was to have a strong influence on Ceri's designs in memory of Dylan.

Caitlin brought Dylan's embalmed body back on the SS *United States* (on which Vernon was to make his first voyage to America eleven years later), and the funeral took place in Laugharne on the twenty-fourth of November. Vernon managed to be present (though with great difficulty, for days off were not easily granted by the bank in those days), but he afterwards felt that it might have been better not to have gone. He very much wanted to see Dylan once more; and the pancake make-up and heavy rouge which Dr Jones refers to would not have bothered him. He would have seen them as one more of the masks that Dylan delighted to wear, and been confident that the real Dylan was there still. But the last look for which he hungered was denied him. Hugh Griffith had hired the car which took him to Laugharne, and felt it essential to stop at every pub on the way in Dylan's honour. When they arrived, the coffin was in the church and the service had started. Later, at the graveside, film and television cameras whirred so loudly that the words of the committal were almost lost. Vernon pushed one camera aside as it obtruded on Caitlin's grief, and its operator hardly troubled to lower his voice as he cursed.

Afterwards, Vernon walked about the little town in the autumn sunshine, but wherever he went he had walked with his friend. When he went back to Pelican, where Dylan's mother lived, she seemed bright, and pleased with the unwonted company and the eulogies of her son. At Brown's afterwards, the atmosphere of hysteria, the squabbles and melodrama, the throwing about of drink, all seemed to him to have nothing to do with Dylan. At one moment, Caitlin leaned her head against his shoulder, and he kissed her gently on the forehead; it seemed to him the saddest moment in a bleak day.

After the funeral there were still memorial programmes; one by the Little Theatre at Bishop Gore Grammar School, at which Vernon read *Portrait of a Friend*, and the much longer one at the Royal Festival Hall on February 14th, at which Michael Hordern read Vernon's *Elegiac Sonnet*. Vernon could not go, and Ceri wrote:

It was an interesting evening, but there were many parts where I felt the sentiment was wrong – the songs, music and singers were wrong and I was indirectly expecting a criticism of this sort from Dan Jones when I asked him if he had found it an interesting evening. But the moment was a wrong one, of course. Perhaps you don't think Dylan's poems are suitable for music settings – and I feel this is true for their content – deeply philosophical and his similes immensely pictorial and visual and the mode of utterance – well his own voice.

Anyway Betty Lutyens doesn't possess the appropriate spirit for it – Edith Evans as a reader was completely out of her depth – although she read the moving oration from Edith Sitwell very nicely. Emlyn W. was good but not so good as in the rehearsal… His 'Visit to Grandpa's' was very good but the 'Just Like Little Dogs' was not so good. R. Burton read Fern Hill very well, obviously he loved this poem and knew it inside out so to speak and that is very important. Edith Evans was a stranger to his work – and Emlyn Williams wasn't deeply moved by it. Hugh Griffith was really Welsh and good – but to listen to the voice of Dylan at the end reading And death shall have no dominion – was perfection proceeded by so much imperfection. That was very moving – very moving. The Excerpt from Milk Wood was very fine – really marvellous…You would have enjoyed the occasion Vernon and I would have liked you to have seen my settings for it – I believe they gave it the right atmosphere – My curtain was in glorification of Dylan and my stage decor more seriously suggesting his passing and flight away from us.

We went to a small party afterwards – I said a word or two to Caitlin who was there. I was in a box with Augustus John but I don't think he could have enjoyed it as he might because he had left his deaf aid behind but he was evidently glad to meet Caitlin.

P. S. Whatever would Dylan say or think if he was able to see what was happening – he would perhaps blow the froth off his celestial beer at us and say we blasphemed – and that we took his name in vain – but he would like it if he feels we do it for love.

Although the news of Dylan's death made a sensation in America and Britain, he was at that time very little known elsewhere (except perhaps in Germany, because of R P Becker's very good translation of *Deaths and Entrances*, called *Tode und Tore.*) That his name was known at all in France was due largely to Francis Dufau-Labeyrie's *Portrait de L'Artiste en Jeune Chien*, and to Vernon's persistent praise of him to Alfred Vallette, whose grandfather founded the *Mercure de France*, and to Georges-Albert Astre, both of whom took care that reviews of Dylan's work appeared in the *Mercure* and in *Lettres Françaises*. Vernon wrote immediately to tell them of Dylan's death. Both were aghast, and Astre replied:

Je suis confus de répondre avec bien du retard a votre longue et émouvante lettre. Oui, j'ai été absolument stupéfait en apprenant la mort de Dylan Thomas... et vraiment ainsi touché par l'évènement que si je l'avais connu, lui, personnellement; j'avais eu l'impression, tellement rare aujourd'hui, d'un poète qui avait inventé un univers (et d'autant plus, je l'avoue, que le 'climat' gallois m'étant moins familier qu'à un critique anglais, j'avais éprouvé tout le choc de ce langage, de cette puissance visionnaire!

Je trouve très regrettable l'ignorance des Français en ce qui concerne Dylan Thomas: mais on le découvrira certainement un jour, dans une dizaine d'années! (C'est toujours ainsi chez nous!)

But no sympathy, no praise of Dylan could help Vernon now. Dylan had gone into that good night he had written of. Ceri understood but could not help. "You must feel a very great emptiness, Vernon, as a fellow poet," he wrote, "and as one who loved his craft and imagery and understood it so deeply, it must be a great loss – a very great loss."

It was indeed – the greatest loss of Vernon's life. Yet, strangely, though others might regret the loss of the poems he would never write, it was the friend of the lost years that he grieved for most.

"The true tragedy of Dylan Thomas's death is that he died," he wrote. "Every other consideration is secondary to that." The poetry remains; it was the vanished past he mourned:

> It is not this that leaves the heart's way ploughed;
> It is the shade the sun no longer flings
> Of one who touched the humble and the proud.

Chapter 13

'TO MOURN THE LATEST DEAD'

You were born to a musical order, die
To a musical order; seek, then, seek
Notes that were true in the past. − V. W.

It can be painful to live up to one's own beliefs. Vernon had always believed that Death is an arbitrary division, and just as a poet writes for the dead, and for the unborn, as much as for the living, the true audience for poetry is found in all three of these categories.

At first, he felt only loss; it was to be years before he came to feel that absence could be as much part of a relationship as presence. He had acknowledged the death of Yeats 'without a change of voice', but the death of Dylan Thomas was to change the voice of his poetry for ever. He would write for Dylan, as he had written for the dead all his poetic life; but also, like Dylan's late poetry, his own would become simpler, plainer, and more conscious of real, rather than literary, sorrow and suffering. The voice of his Muse had aged.

His verse had always moved to an elegiac tone: this, he said, was something over which he had no control. The material for poetry 'came' to him; except in the case of light or humorous verse, he could not choose it. (He left hundreds of unfinished poems, often with a hundred or more drafts − never finished because they were poems he had wanted to write, but for which his Muse did not choose to 'send' the material). In the years after Dylan's death, poem after poem welled from his imagination like blood from a wound. The old intimacy might have ended in life, but it had never ended in Vernon's heart, and his marvellous memory ('old Datas Watkins') re-created every incident and word of the past, as though it were still the present.

The first of the Dylan poems, evidently begun very soon after his death, since it was published in May 1954, in *Botteghe Oscure*, was *Elegy For the Latest Dead*. It was a short sonnet sequence, which in early drafts consists of five sonnets, each with its own title. The first sonnet is a meditation over the poet's grave; the second has moved with the curlew to the Gower cliffs, where the friends so often met. The third and fourth sonnets recall those meetings.

> When first we met, this is the path we took,
> Exchanging thought, when, with a sudden look,
> He showed Earth shining like an open page,
> A myth in his live hand too young for age.
>
> His stubborn zeal transformed archaic skill,
> Binding young words old courses to fulfil
> Held by the curb of his unvarying soul
> Which kept all majesty in pure control
> While each excursion gave them fiery blood.
>
> Above this path, high on the cliff we stood
> That day, competing who could further cast
> A knife-edged stone. That knife-edge whistling past,
> Singing through air, hit rocks and water now.
> He crouched, and listened for the scream below.
>
> If the wrong world, if man's abuse of man
> Cast his own shadow on the race he ran,
> Here he forgot it. Here above the slade
> Sprang to immediate life his talking shade,
> The forward-looking shade accompanied
> By all the imagination in its greed
> Which, on the long, bare cliff-walks we enjoyed,
> With living shapes would dramatize the void.
>
> And I recall one late October day
> When, going to bathe, he peopled the whole bay
> (It was already dark) with human brutes

> Feeding in silence, in correct grey suits,
> Compact and patient, one with sanguine sighs
> Offering the next a sandwich of dried eyes.

And, in spite of the momentary lift of the heart at the recollection of Dylan's comic fantasizing, the sequence ends in almost pure sorrow.

> Yet, though all faded, still I count it pure
> To have loved the valid fact, made that endure
> Which held his heart and fixed the heron's eye.
> Who now says nothing says as much as I.
> Whatever books men write, when all is said
> There are no words to mourn the latest dead.

In April 1954, the son who was to have been Dylan's godchild was born. The only way in which Vernon could attempt to resolve the poignancy of his joy and pain was by making verse. It was, that year, an early and heart-breakingly lovely spring. Already at the beginning of April, the apple-blossom was in bud and the fragile beech-leaves were breaking. The woodpecker darted shouting about the garden for days, as Vernon watched his new-born child sleeping. This was the source of the poem, *Birth and Morning*. The final version breathes through all its twelve verses a sense of bitter loss.

> I restore to the garden the footprints of one that was near
> Whose arms would cradle you now, a magnanimous ghost,
> But who sleeps without knowing your name in the turn and the quick
> of the year.

An earlier draft, now in the British Library, is yet more piercing.

> Who then, shall wake them, these the heart held dear?
> Of the many whose names are in the dust,
> Of the one I shall name him by,
>
> While the apple-trees move under wind in the wonder of morning,
> He nothing knows. Now the woodpecker, knocking, is near,
> But he does not hear, and a tear is all I know, or he, of the sky.

Another draft expresses not only grief, but the isolation of the grieving.

> That lies in earth about which the air knows nothing.
> In the dark there sleeps that which could tell the light,
> But those about me ignore it;

These things are beautiful in themselves;
They remember nothing;
They exist in the mind of God,
Nor grieve for that which is lost.

Birth and Morning forms part of Vernon's fifth book of poems, which appeared six years after Dylan's death. The title, *Cypress and Acacia*, explains its theme; the cypress is the tree of death, the acacia of life. The whole book is a meditation on the meaning of death to the living. Many of its poems are concerned, explicitly or implicitly, with the death of Dylan Thomas. *The Curlew* is one of the most moving of these; originally one of the sonnets in the sequence *Elegy For the Latest Dead*, it turned into a poem in its own right.

Sweet-throated cry, by one no longer heard
Who, more than many, loved the wandering bird,
Unchanged through generations and renewed,
Perpetual child of its own solitude,
The same on rocks and over sea I hear
Return now with his unreturning year.

In the earlier sonnet these lines were more poignant still.

Alone I hear it now, alone I hear
A curlew call the unreturning year.

A group of these poems, *The Sloe, The Return,* and *The Exacting Ghost*, describe the effect on Vernon of a dream about Dylan, which came to him in, I think, February or early March of 1954. It caused him great uneasiness, because, unlike most dreams, it had a quality of extreme reality. Every outline appeared solid; he could see the texture of Dylan's skin and the slightly greasy gloss on his hair, as though he were looking at a film close-up. He even saw a small mole on the side of the jaw, which he did not remember having seen in Dylan's lifetime. Vernon was neither a superstitious nor an impressible man (he once said that he could not imagine being afraid of ghosts), but he was never able to decide whether this was an unusually vivid dream or an actual visit from the dead.

The Sloe, which was the earliest of the three poems, describes the strange sensation of the dreamer seeing the dead friend's face with greater clarity than it was ever seen in life.

> Too like those lineaments
> For waking eyes to see,
> Yet those the dream presents
> Clearly to me.

> How much more vivid now
> Than when across your tomb
> Sunlight projects a bough
> In gradual gloom.

This was evidently not enough to exorcise the dream's power, nor, indeed, was the next poem, *The Return*. This is a disturbing poem, comparing the atmosphere of the dream to the terror of an air-raid. Its original title, when it was first published in *The London Magazine*, in May 1955, was *The Return (of a dead friend who experienced an air-raid with me)*.

> I lay, pulse beating fast,
> While the night-raider passed
> And gave each hovering tick
> The speed of dream.
> Sleep in the dead of night could make all quick,
> Reverse the extreme
> Outrider's task on thought's magnetic beam.

> What life-uprooting year
> Sent him, an envoy, here
> To set two states at war?
> I'ld rather set
> Those just names up both states are honoured for,
> Lest time forget
> He is a hostage since our eyes last met.

> Now from that neighbour state
> One who all war did hate
> Came as a witness back
> From that night raid,
> To make a truce, there in the very track
> Where wings had made
> A single engine stop, two hearts afraid.

But the end of the poem finds the 'two states' still unreconciled.

> Why let two states at war
> Destroy the mind?
> Those eyes beneath a brutal metaphor
> Can substance find
> In all time spurns but cannot leave behind.

The long struggle to resolve the dichotomies of life and death, good and evil, dark and light was, much later, to take shape in the dramatic poem, *The Ballad of the Outer Dark*, a sequel to *Ballad of the Mari Lwyd*. But when the two dream-poems left him still restless and uneasy, Vernon wrote a third, the kind of poem he had not written since that other poem of a dead friend, *Yeats in Dublin*: a plainly factual, almost a narrative account. This was *The Exacting Ghost*.

> I speak of an exacting ghost,
> And if the world distrust my theme
> I answer: this that moved me most
> Was first a vision, then a dream.
>
> By the new year you set great store.
> The leaves are turned, and some are shed.
> A sacred, moving metaphor
> Is living in my mind, though dead.
>
> I would have counted good years more,
> But all is changed: your life is set.
> I praise that living metaphor
> And when I sleep I see it yet...
>
> In crowded tavern you I found
> Conversing there, yet knew you dead.
> This was no ghost. When you turned round
> It was indeed your living head.
>
> Time had returned, and pregnant wit
> Lodged in your eyes. What health was this?
> Never had context been so fit
> To give old words new emphasis.

If hope was then restrained by doubt
Or joy by fear, I cannot tell.
All the disturbances of thought
Hung on my words, yet all seemed well.

You smiled. Your reassurance gave
My doubt its death, my hope its due.
I had always known beyond the grave,
I said, all would be well with you.

You fixed contracted, narrowing eyes
To challenge my instinctive sense,
The uncertainty of my surmise
Their penetration made intense.

'What right had you to know, what right
To arrogate so great a gift?'
I woke, and memory with the light
Brought back a weight I could not lift.

In sleep the dead and living year
Had stood one moment reconciled,
But in the next the accuser's spear
Had sacked the city of the child.

When Vernon was a young poet, he had written, in *A Prayer Against Time*:

God, let me not know grief
Where time is uppermost,
Not though it handle me
More wretchedly than all...

Now he was suffering grief in which time seemed to be uppermost. There had been a time when Dylan was alive, then came a moment out of time, the moment of his death, and then a time when all was 'changed, changed utterly', but a time that had to be lived through. Vernon was a Christian, he believed in the immortality of the soul and certainly in the immortality of Dylan's verse; but still – something had changed.

There has passed away a glory from the earth.

The knowledge that Dylan was alive and writing had been very precious to Vernon, and now he had to live without that knowledge. What, after all, do we know about life after death? *Angel and Man* expresses that uncertainty. The Angel promises that:

> All sighs are ended.
> The sleep of earth, the long night sleep is over.

But the risen man rejects the promise.

> I would believe you but I cannot.
> Too much is hidden.
> I hear your speech, but when your speech has faded
> It is the earth that counts, where these men lived...
> ...Let others be deceived.
> I know this for a place where footsteps halted
> And where each footstep knocked upon the ground,
> Seeking true consolation. Think of this.
> Spirits were laid here to whom some were dear,
> Who left them, sorrowful...
> I accept this for my portion. Grief was theirs,
> And grief, their lot, is likely to be mine.

The Mask of Winter, too, is a poem which seems to equate winter with loss, and to find remote the promise of an eventual spring.

> Until the waking bud
> Forms on the sleeping tree,
> By dictates of the blood
> The dead admonish me.
>
> I cannot separate
> So soundlessly they shine,
> The windings of past fate,
> Nor the lost lives from mine.
>
> Yet nowhere in this waste
> Voices from time endure.
> No footprint here is traced,
> No dying signature.
>
> No rain, no curlew-cry
> Calling across the field:

> The locked lane under sky
> Is blocked with snow and sealed.

Again, in *Buried Light*, loss seems paramount, and consolation not to be considered.

> What are the light and wind to me?
> The lamp I love is gone to ground.
> There all the thunder of the sea
> Becomes by contrast idle sound...
> And men may find, beneath the sun,
> Dashed into pieces by old wrong,
> A relic, lost to nature, one
> Whose passion stops the mouth of song.

The same sense of utter loss shows in the last verse of a three-verse typescript, found, with many other drafts of poems for Dylan, after Vernon's own death.

> Who would have thought a single step
> And voice could widow all the ground
> And bring a garland to my sleep
> Brighter than all the day had found?

In the Protestant Cemetery, Rome (whose first line, 'Where Cypress and Acacia Stand,' gives the book its title) is not explicitly concerned with Dylan's death, but there is no doubt that this was in Vernon's mind when he wrote it. The poem describes the graves of Keats and Shelley, each neighboured by the grave of a friend, Severn and Trelawney.

> And the paired friends, a space apart,
> Draw the leaves' whisperings, heart to heart.

It is impossible that Vernon should not have thought of his own friend's grave. These lines seem to me to be as much about that Laugharne churchyard as about Rome.

> How still the graveyard: one at peace
> And one so restless. Time must cease
> Before they understand each other.
> Yet now they do, for now their mother
> Casts on them her falling leaves.
> No longer the miraculous grieves

For youth cut off, reclaimed by age,
Where history sets a tragic stage.

Character keeps its vesture on
Holding the body, though it's gone;
And the paired friends, a space apart,
Draw the leaves' whisperings, heart to heart.

After Dylan's death, the myth machine gathered speed and rattled across America and Britain for the next ten years. Sometimes the freight it carried was a grubby one. Dylan, said *Time* magazine, was:

... a slob, a liar, a moocher, a thief, a two-fisted booze-fighter, a puffy Priapus who regularly assaulted the wives of his best friends, an icy little hedonist who indifferently lived it up while his children went hungry... Though he looked like a choirboy, he argued like a Bolshevik, dressed like a bum, drank like a culvert, smoked like an ad for cancer, bragged that he was addicted to onanism and had committed an indecency with a member of parliament.

Dispiriting though such stuff was to read, it was no worse than the over-sentimentalised reminiscences of people who had once stood next to him in a bar or seen him standing on the opposite platform in a railway station. John Ciardi commented on the strange phenomenon of Dylan's power to create a sense of intimacy in everyone he met.

...the country is sown from coast to coast with people who honestly think of him as an intimate friend, usually after no more than one or two drinks together. Something about the man involved people in him.

The picture of Dylan presented by both admirers and detractors seemed to Vernon more and more unlike the man he had known; the poet seemed to be forgotten in anecdotes of the drunkard and entertainer. It was not so much indignation that a life should be cheapened, since Dylan never minded being misunderstood, and indeed often gleefully brought about deliberate misunderstandings, that led to the poem *A True Picture Restored*.

Composed in 1954, it was a noble vindication, not of the poetry, which needed no vindication, but of the man whose life had been devoted to its creation. Dylan is given his rightful place with the great poets he loved.

> Nearer the pulse than other themes
> His deathborn claims are pressed.
> Fired first by Milton, then the dreams
> Of Herbert's holy breast,
> Out of his days the sunlight streams
> And fills the burning West.

> I look where soon the frosty Plough
> Shall hang above the sill
> And see the colours westward flow
> To green Carmarthen's hill.
> There sinks the sky of changes now
> On waters never still.

> Praise God, although a time is gone
> That shall not come again,
> If ever morning rightly shone,
> A glass to make all plain,
> The man I mourn can make it live,
> Every fallen grain.

The poem restores the 'true picture' by painting lovingly remembered scenes from the house in Cwmdonkin Drive, from Sea View and Laugharne, and from wartime London. There are oblique references to *The Hunchback in the Park, Prologue, Over Sir John's Hill* and *Under Milk Wood*; but, on the whole, the tone is entirely personal. The bitter regret is for the man, not his work, and it ends as it began, firmly rooted in Wales.

> Let each whose soul is in one place
> Still to that place be true.
> The man I mourn could honour such
> With every breath he drew.
> I never heard him wish to take
> A life from where it grew.

And yet the man I mourn is gone,
He who could give the rest
So much to live for till the grave,
And do it all in jest.
Hard it must be, beyond this day,
For even the grass to rest.

It is a *tour de force*, and was received as such when *Affinities* was published in 1962. One critic said:

The poem has a ringing authenticity and a sense of awe which sets Dylan once and for all above the trivia of the Dylanolaters and the academic assertions of the Dylanologists.

Louise Bogan, herself a poet of considerable stature, wrote in the *New Yorker*:

Watkins steps into one well-lit center of contemporary interest with a long, beautifully written and most poignant elegy... As Thomas's fellow-poet, compatriot and elder friend, Watkins describes the virtues of a young Thomas as they have never before been described.

The poem was also in some sense a catalyst for Vernon's feelings about Dylan's death. He still, and always, missed him and grieved for him, he continually wrote and talked about him, he was to write other poems about him, but never again one so personal, so intimately concerned with a shared past. Even *The Shell*, sad though it is, expresses its sadness in metaphor.

Rollie McKenna, the American photographer, had given Vernon a photograph of Dylan, which he kept always standing on his worktable. He wrote a poem about it, *The Present*, which describes the difficulty of synthesising the past, present and future times. Again, the poem is sorrowful, but with a muted sorrow.

Strange, is it not, that he for whom
The living moment stood in flesh,
Should bring the future to this room
Held at arm's length, and always fresh.

Strange, that his echoing words can spell
New meanings though the die is cast,
And tell us more than time can tell,
Immediate in a timeless Past;

And stranger still, for us who knew
The living face and now return
Its pictured gaze, so quick, so new,
Love's vital fire being its concern,

To think, though years should gallop now
Or lag behind, he will not care,
So calm the eyes beneath the brow,
Held in a breath by angels there.

To the end of Vernon's life, the shade of Dylan Thomas continued to haunt his poems. In an early poem he had said: "For the dead live, and I am of their kind."

It became, in a way, true. He loved life, but half of his thoughts were with the dead, and the past was as real to him as the present.

His name being said, instantly he appears,
Caught, in a timeless flash, with life's own look
Which none could seize or copy in a book.
I marvel, who had missed that look for years.

The making and cheapening of the Dylan legend he always scorned, and out of his scorn made the bitter little poem *Exegesis*.

So many voices
Instead of one.
Light, that is the driving force
Of song alone:
Give me this or darkness,
The man or his bone.

None shall replace him,
Only falsify
Light broken into colours,
The altered sky.
Hold back the bridle,
Or the truth will lie.

But even grief has its death and, though the sky be for ever altered, it has its resurrection. The first poem that Vernon had written in Dylan's memory was a curlew elegy, in which the bird's call carried remorse across the sea, and, itself returning, recalled the one who would never return. Now, at last, towards the end of his own life (the poem appeared 'in the posthumous *Fidelities*), he wrote another curlew poem. Here the call foretells the end of winter, and the poet is left, as the cry fades, to his work of creation. The poem is called *The Snow Curlew*.

> Snow has fallen all night
> Over the cliffs. There are no paths.
> All is even and white.
> The leaden sea ebbs back, the sky is not yet light.
> Hidden from dawn's grey patch
> Behind frosted windows, ash ticks out faded hearths.
>
> How quietly time passes. There is no mark
> Yet upon this manuscript of snow.
> Where water dripped, ice glitters, sheaved and stark.
> The pen has fallen from the hand of dark.
> White are lintel and latch.
> Earth has forgotten where her dead go.
>
> Silence. Then a curlew flutes with its cry,
> The low distance, that throbbing spring call,
> Swifter than thought. It is goodbye
> To all things not beginning, and I must try,
> Making the driftwood catch,
> To coax, where the cry fades, fires which cannot fall.

Photograph by Rollie McKenna

So calm the eyes beneath the brow
Held in a breath by angels there.

Chapter 14

A TRUE PICTURE RESTORED

Time has no present till the past is true. – V. W.

Vernon was to labour all his life to restore what he believed to be the 'true picture' of his dead friend, but, except for the scripts that he wrote for the many talks he gave on Dylan's poetry, he took it for granted that his labours would always be in verse. He thought that poetry was the language of belief and praise, while prose was the language of speculation, argument and rhetoric, for none of which he had much use. Dylan, however, evidently still exercised from beyond the grave his former powers of drawing his friends into his own orbit, and embroiling them in unwished for activities. Vernon found himself increasingly involved in undesired controversies, as counsel for the defence in literary indictments, as reluctant protagonist in arguments he disliked and resented.

The first spate of reminiscences about Dylan was beginning to die down when John Malcolm Brinnin's *Dylan Thomas in America* was published in 1956. It is difficult now to understand the hurricane of recrimination, protest and abuse raised by this inaccurate but fairly harmless book. To Vernon, as to many of Dylan's friends who had known him much longer than Brinnin, it was a betrayal of the truth about him, and Brinnin became Judas to a Christ-like Dylan. Vernon was sent the book for review. He was in a dilemma. He had always refused to review books by living authors, but he did not wish to lose the opportunity to say something about the book which he thought ought to be said, and which, so far, had not been said. He compromised by writing, at Stephen Spender's request, a non-review, an article entitled *Dylan Thomas in America* (published in *Encounter*), which made his views of Brinnin very clear indeed. An unpublished draft makes them clearer still.

I was recently sent John Malcolm Brinnin's book for review, but declined, because I do not review books by living authors. Had I accepted, I would have been bound to condemn the book, in which I recognise two values only, the quoted words and judgments of Dylan Thomas himself and the narration, in the last chapter, of the circumstances which led to his death. To call that death a self-inflicted one by any standards, and particularly by moral ones, is to accept the superficial tone in which the book is written, is itself the hallmark of a superficial acquaintance and prime evidence that its author did not know the man.

• • •

The tragedy of Dylan Thomas's death is made more bitter by the banality of judgment to which it gives rise. Those who were magnetised by his power to entertain became the victims of a mutually enacted delusion. The poet, simple, unaffected and true, was a person rarely seen by his audience, whose dramatic spotlight changed him into what they desired. His stories, his wise-cracks, they remembered, as who would not? But the surprising consistency of his judgments is one thing they never seem to have observed. In America his audiences recognised the superb reader of poetry certainly, but of the poet himself they knew nothing, or at least that is the impression left by this book. It might almost be said that he was killed partly by the grimace which responded to his entertainment and partly by the lack of any face which could see through it.

To anyone who grasps this tragedy, whose final scene is horribly accelerated like a nightmare of misinterpretations on many levels, can anything be more cheap, tawdry and irrelevant than the carefully rendered account of everything the poet ate, or didn't eat, and drank? Can anything have less interest for any man on earth than the particular domestic scenes in which the author of the book exhibits the object of his mistaken idolatry to the curiosity of the world? It is certain that Dylan Thomas adapted his behaviour to his company, that he was willing to go a long way with any man in his imagination to explore that world, provided that it did not bore or disgust him. His instinct in conversation was to give, and to give prodigiously, and this instinct never failed.

• • •

To imagine Dylan Thomas as a teetotaller is a sad picture, and this he would not have become, but he was not an alcoholic either. Beer was to him a necessary social medium. Spirits were not, and it is my belief that this unnecessary social adjunct, which is the medium of American hospitality, hastened his death.

It would be comforting, I suppose, for some people to regard his record-breaking bout of spirit-drinking just before his death as a climax, a vindication of art against the world. Yet nothing could be further from the truth. Those who treasure such a misconception of the artist are likely to misunderstand any artist, but particularly this one. It is their picture that is emasculated, not he, and it is to their picture that he has succumbed. His death is the death they would expect of such an artist, but his death is also, on other terms, his own death, and therein lies the tragedy.

A minor surprise of Brinnin's book is the almost complete absence from its pages of the people about whom Dylan Thomas was most eloquent when he returned from the tours. His enthusiasm for certain poets whose names hardly occur in the narrative had made the tours worth while. Everyone who reads this book should know that at least one other book, even on this subject, has been left out. His widow's introduction is sufficient to put readers on their guard.

Besides this, there is an axiom that it is never possible to explain a poet's life. It is least of all possible in the eyes of one who builds upon the slender foundations of a late, business-distorted encounter. The eyes of a deceived photographer necessarily prepare the artificial pose. He sells to the world, without knowing it, a picture, or pictures, of a person who does not exist.

The poetry of Dylan Thomas and his late prose will remain his best interpreter. To the professional interrogator the task of meeting him involved the removal of many masks. He was himself stubborn, dogged and constant, fiery, combative, full of wonder, self-critical, compassionate, generous, trusting simplicity through every complexity of mind, sociable, glad of company, absorbed in all the mystery and extension of immediate experience. He was also extremely witty, and out of a fundamental honesty drew, at any desired moment, enough extravagance to illustrate his own myth. Even when the myth possessed him he remained true to the values of his imagination. Had he compromised with opposing values he might, imaginatively, have had everything to die for; instead he had everything to live for, when he died.

The article was exceptionally personal. Vernon was revealing a man hardly anyone else knew – the young poet and iconoclast who had revealed himself to a fellow poet. The impression these revelations made on him was so strong that he found it difficult to accept that there were sides to Dylan he did not know. But certainly, Brinnin knew much less, in every sense, than Vernon, who was right to distrust the so-called facts in Brinnin's book – even when they were accepted as true by most readers at that time. If he had lived, he would have learned with relief that the accounts of Dylan's last weeks depended, not on Brinnin, who was not with Dylan, but on the accounts of Elizabeth Reitell, generally agreed to be a most unreliable witness. I find it difficult to believe in Brinnin's stories, too; when I was in America I met people who gave me quite different accounts of some of the New York parties. But apart from any of Brinnin's other statements, no-one who actually knew Dylan could believe that he ever held Brinnin 'very firmly' from behind and said, "John, you know, don't you? – this is for ever." If he did actually do and say this, it must have been with a Noel Cowardish, courageous look, reminiscent of his Little Theatre days; but he was behind Brinnin, who could not see his 'taking the Mickey'. There is no way that Dylan Thomas, rigorous tester of language, could ever say, "You know this is for ever," – words from any soap opera – without grinning.

It would have given Vernon grave pleasure, too, to know that very few people at the present day believe that alcohol was the cause of Dylan's death. Whether the cause was untreated diabetes or Dr Feltenstein's 'twinkling needle', it was not a self-inflicted death. But at that time, he could not help feeling bitterly about *Dylan Thomas in America* and its author: but, to remind himself of his own picture of Dylan, he assembled all Dylan's letters to him and read them through for the first time since the death. It was now that he conceived the idea of publishing them. He had resisted all attempts by American dealers to buy them (one attempt to steal them was unsuccessful), and had never had any intention of making them public. But on re-reading them, he became convinced that there was in them a great deal of material that would be of the greatest value to scholars and lovers of Dylan's poetry. Still undecided, he submitted the letters to T. S. Eliot for an unbiased opinion. Both Eliot and Charles Monteith felt that they should be published, and Vernon asked the Trustees of the Dylan Thomas Estate for their permission. The Trustees replied that permission would be granted only on condition that the book should be brought out by Dylan's own publishers, Dent. Vernon dug in his heels immediately; any firm which had published Brinnin's book, he said, should never publish the letters he owned. There was a complete impasse.

But Dent wanted very much to publish the letters. David Higham, Dylan's agent and one of the Trustees, wrote to Vernon on April 23, 1956:

I saw Stuart last week and he told me he had discussed with you my letter to him. I understand from him that you assented generally to the views I expressed, but feel reluctant about letting Dent have the book for the simple reason that they are publishing Brinnin's book.

... When this book by Brinnin came into my hands I had to recognise that no one had the power to stop its publication. In America it could be published without regard to any law of libel as we understand it and even here only minor modifications have been made, to make the book safe for a publisher who was prepared to take a reasonable risk of action. On the other hand, the book did and does contain a few pieces of work, which are Dylan's copyright, which are useful to it. I saw the opportunity for obtaining an assurance from the publishers here and in America that they would print the book with a disclaimer by Caitlin at the start. I also made quite sure that Caitlin should see the book before any further step was taken, and she did in fact read it and assented to its publication provided that her disclaimer was printed with it... We even secured that this disclaimer should be printed with the extracts used serially in America. It seemed to me that if the book was to be published here, and we could not possibly prevent it being published, it was far better for Dent's to have it, since, as Dylan's own publishers, they would handle it with far more dignity and restraint than any other house... I believe that to permit this publication is the right policy... If we as Dylan's Trustees – and of course I consulted the others – make any effort to suppress what someone thinks is the truth about Dylan there will inevitably arise rumours that there is something to be suppressed. The result of the publication of this book is going to be, you know, the exposure of Brinnin rather than Dylan to the public view, and in the interests of truth I think that is no bad thing, do you?... But whatever you think of the Trustees' policy, it is no more than fair to Dent that I should explain how they come into it. I think, whatever views you may have, you must hold them blameless. Let me hear what you think, and whether you now believe we could go ahead with Dylan's letters to you and with Dent. I quite understand that your sending them to Eliot was in no sense an offer to Faber but merely a submission to him personally.

But Vernon was unconvinced. On April 24 he replied:

I am quite sure that in deciding to accept Brinnin's book for publication by Dent...you acted with the best of motives... I was, however, shocked that in this country it should be accepted by the same publishers who printed the COLLECTED POEMS. My own instinct would have been to turn it down, not on the grounds of suppressing the truth, but on the grounds of its total inability to state it. You are right in saying that I sent the letters to Eliot as a matter of personal interest, and not with a view to early publication. I did, at the same time, want to know whether in his opinion they would form a self-contained book, as I realised that sooner or later a decision about this would have to be made; and I thought that his opinion, as a person of great judgment and not particularly predisposed to favour Dylan's work, would be valuable. He did appreciate the letters, at first with some reservation, but later, I think, with complete enthusiasm, and Charles Monteith agreed with him that they would form an excellent book.

The position, therefore, is this: Faber's have taken up the suggestion of printing these letters as a separate book, and, rather to my surprise, they would like to publish them soon. To this I am agreeable. Such a separate publication before a definitive edition of letters by the regular publisher has many precedents, the most recent perhaps being Yeats' *Letters to Dorothy Wellesley*, published by the Oxford Press before the Macmillan edition...

Faber's are in my view the best publishers for the book. The book is already virtually accepted by them, subject to the approval of the Trustees. If the Trustees are not willing to let Faber's have the book, there remain two alternatives: either the letters are not to be published at all, or they may be offered to Dent's at some future time. I am quite agreeable to the first alternative. The publication of Brinnin's book has compelled me to oppose the second. I have quite made up my mind about this. Faber's may have the book now. If they do not, Dent's will not have it until some time after their own book of miscellaneous letters has appeared.

All three parties now stood firm, each on his own strong point – Vernon, that he would not release the letters except to Faber; the Trustees, that they would give permission for publication only to Dent; and Faber, that Vernon would release the letters only to them. The cold war continued for many months, but eventually a kind of thaw set in, proceeding naturally enough from Faber and Dent, who were both extremely anxious to publish the letters. On 18 December 1956, Peter du Sautoy, one of Faber's directors, wrote to Vernon:

> We are on the point of concluding agreements both with Dents and with the Dylan Thomas Trustees for the publication of Dylan Thomas's letters to you... the publication to be a joint one over the imprint of Dent and ourselves.
>
> You may have heard the arrangements that we have made with Dents. We are going to produce the book and they are going to be responsible for selling it. Of course we shall each of us announce it in our own catalogues, but it seems best to have that division of labour which is clear and straightforward.

There seemed no reason not to agree with this plan, and the typescript was immediately sent to Faber, who passed it to Dent for a libel report. This again gave rise to several bursts of correspondence, which Dylan would greatly have enjoyed.

The libel report itself makes splendid comic reading. Dent's lawyer expressed anxiety about Dylan's hostess in Cornwall (Wyn Henderson) being described as 'a simple person', and about the military policemen drinking with the soldiers they had been sent to arrest.

He was also worried about Dylan's descriptions of 'Alfred Janes's deficiencies as a letter-writer.' ("...now I have decided to abandon the book I was going to write and devote myself to the Life and Letter of Alfred Janes.") He was worried about John Davenport being called an 'amateur' writer. So was John Davenport. He wrote forcefully to Vernon.

> The nineteen stone (17, actually), the musicianship, the *etc.* are all fine. It's the 'amateur' that galls. 'Bad' would be better, if less flattering. It was the fact that I was in the strict sense a professional writer that enabled me to keep Dylan and his family for six months. Failed poets become professional writers, like me; Dylan, God bless him, was the amateur.

Mr Grey Morgan, former headmaster of the Grammar School, had to be asked whether he objected to Dylan's letter of March 16, 1947. ("...I had to go and see a master... to find out how much of the school was burned. 'Bloody near all,' he said, then with a nasty sigh, he added, 'All except Grey Morgan.') The old man replied forgivingly. "The anecdote is new to me. I was 'tickled' and enjoyed the joke. To intimates, it is a typical Dylan "leg-pull" and I cannot object to it in isolation... Your letter brought back dim memories of fixing up Dylan in his first job at the *Evening Post!*"

A more serious matter was Dylan's account of the machine-gun attack at Newquay. Vernon wanted to print the complete letter, on the ground that the affair had been fully reported in the daily papers at the time of the attacker's trial. Dent and Faber were not so sanguine, Charles Monteith explained what was worrying them.

> Quite apart from the libel danger, don't you think it might be a good idea, on general grounds of letting bygones to some extent be bygones to suppress Killick's name?...Technically, of course, this would hardly diminish the libel risk at all, though in practice it might very effectively reduce it, for the institution of proceedings by Killick would inevitably result in fresh publicity about this affair, in which his name couldn't be suppressed. What is important is that you should satisfy yourself that Dylan Thomas's account of what happened is, in fact, an accurate one. I've no reason at all to suppose that it isn't, but it might possibly be that the story which was eventually established in court differed in some particulars from D. T.'s narrative in his letter.

It was not until Vernon had done a great deal of research – work which was very uncongenial to him – that Monteith wrote again, to say that Mr Bozman of Dent and he had changed their minds.

> Here I've got to pass on what will, I fear, seem a pusillanimous opinion – but it is the unanimous and firmly held opinion of Bozman and myself. We both think that all references to this case should be cut out completely. The reason for my change of view is that I didn't realise until I read the press cutting which you sent me that Killick had been acquitted. From charges of (a) attempted murder (b) firing with intent to endanger life (c) of having intended to commit bodily harm, a jury completely exonerated him, and I've little doubt that Dylan Thomas's letter would be held to constitute a repetition of these charges which the prosecution failed to establish... If you yourself should feel strongly that the passage should be retained we could go back to the libel lawyer for his further advice. I've very little doubt, though, that his advice would be in favour of deletion. It's a tremendous pity that the passage should go, – it's lively, exciting

and of the greatest possible biographical interest; it isn't, though, directly relevant – is it? – to the shaping or evolution of any of Dylan Thomas's poems.

Vernon wearily wrote to Mrs Killick, whom he had known slightly when she was Vera Phillips, only to find that she was now separated from her husband. He managed, however, to contact this gentleman, who, naturally enough, wanted the whole affair to be forgotten and every reference to it omitted from the book. Vernon felt that this would make the whole letter meaningless, but Bozman and the libel lawyer wanted the whole letter dropped. It took many letters and telephone calls to bring everyone concerned to an agreement that the passage in question should read:

> I'd have written before this but… Caitlin and I go to bed under the bed.

This was *not* a satisfactory solution. It was, perhaps, the best that could be done, but Vernon felt that an enormous expenditure of time and energy had achieved very little. He was also embroiled in a correspondence with Lynette Roberts, former wife of Keidrych Rhys, who passionately objected to a paragraph about herself which said:

> Lynette, who cannot read Welsh, is revising the standard nineteenth-century book on Welsh Prosody, and also annotating a work on the Hedgerows of Carmarthenshire. I hope she becomes famous, and that they will name an insect after her.

To avoid more indignant letters, Vernon cravenly yielded and left out the entire paragraph. But he was becoming exhausted and exasperated. He had thought that he would need only to type, annotate and arrange the letters, and to write a foreword, but for almost ten months he had not been able to work on his own poetry, for which continuity was essential. He began to wish that he had never embarked on the project. He had so little free time, and he did not want to spend what he had in the kind of altercation and discussion of business detail which he detested.

At last, however, the galley proofs had been corrected, the page-proofs were actually being set, and Vernon felt that he could begin to write poetry again, when something happened that almost resulted in the withdrawal from publication of the letters at the last moment. David Higham, who, besides being one of the Trustees, was also Dylan's agent, had arranged with Dent and Faber that they should offer a royalty of 12½% of the published price on up to 4,000 copies, and 15% thereafter, with an advance on royalties of £300 – £100 on signature and £200 on publication. Higham's letter to Vernon in November 1956, explaining these arrangements, went on:

> The Trustees propose that this first £100 should be paid to you in full, they to receive the £200 when the book comes out.

Vernon had agreed to this, but when, in February, the cheque for the advance arrived, it was for £90 only; Pearn, Pollinger and Higham had deducted their 10% commission. All Vernon's pent-up exasperation exploded in fury. He withdrew the letters from publication. The £10 was nothing, but that Dylan's agent should take a commission for doing nothing to help him (and Higham was not, after all, his agent) was too much. Nobody, not even Higham himself, could offer any reason why he should take this commission, but he refused to budge. It would, after all, be Vernon's own publishers who would suffer, not Dent, since they had undertaken production, and would have to pay for all that had been done up to and including the page-proofs, and this was what Higham relied on. Vernon insisted on an agreement with Higham that he was free to reprint his own Foreword to the book without the deduction of an agent's commission. He was not a resentful man, but all his life he resented this unjust action of Higham's for so petty a sum.

There was, however, one small circumstance connected with the publication of the letters that always gave Vernon unfailing pleasure. Dent was in some ways an unlikely publisher for Dylan, since, as a house, it was inclined to be careful, if not actually prudish. Richard Church, Dent's adviser, confessed that he found Dylan's poetry 'alarming', and,

indeed, refused to include *A Prospect of the Sea* in *The Map of Love* because
of its 'unwarrantable moments of sensuality'. It seemed likely then that,
since Dylan's letters were much more outspoken than anything he wrote
for publication, a good deal even of what was left after the libel lawyer
had been through it would be censored. But, in fact, Mr Bozman, an
anxious but charming elderly gentleman, allowed such explicit passages as
'...the dogs piss only on backdoors, and there are more unwanted babies
shoved up the chimneys than there are used french letters in the offertory
boxes', but stuck, inexplicably, at the word 'shit'. Not only would he not
allow the word to be printed, but he evidently found himself unable to
enunciate it. Telephone communications from Bozman about 'that word'
were passed on almost daily by Charles Monteith. A typical bulletin in
January 1957 read:

> *That word*. I've spoken to Bozman on the telephone about this
> and his own strongly held view is that 'the whole passage' should
> be deleted... I think what he means is that the words 'I bow
> before shit' should be taken out *in toto*. Though I'm sorry about
> this, and personally should be in favour of leaving them in, my
> own view is that it's too trivial to make a fuss about and that we
> should agree. My original impression was that Dents would be
> quite happy with 'sh-t', but apparently that was wrong.

But, trivial or not, the controversy raged on, until Vernon, amused and
compassionate at Bozman's crescendo of agitation, allowed the word to
be deleted. *Letters to Vernon Watkins* came out in the autumn of 1957.
This book has become a vital part of the critical equipment of every
Dylan Thomas student, but the initial reviews were poor; no British critic
appeared to realise the importance of the letters. And these brought out, as
Dylan himself brought out, all sorts of strange reactions. Richard Church
(whom Dylan greatly disliked) talked only of his own dealings with the
poet, including his once borrowing half-a-crown: "In the circumstances,
it was embarrassing." All he said of the book of letters, in a review of two
and a half columns in *Truth*, was, "Meanwhile, here are his charming

letters from his old friend Watkins." Stephen Spender, in two columns in the *Observer*, ran down Dylan's character, poetry and letters – in a curious review that seemed to be motivated entirely by envy and dislike. Of Dylan's character, he said:

> Acquire a reputation for borrowing money, getting drunk, sleeping around, and do any or all of these things for any and all. It saves time and answers so many questions that it prevents the real questions being asked.

Of the poems he said:

> … with all the fullness of his rhetorical language, and despite his passionate mourning and praise, there were unexplained empty gulfs in Thomas…. One could scarcely make a prose paraphrase of what is said in a Dylan Thomas poem without an almost total loss of what the poem means.

(Vernon would have said that this was true of any great poem. If the poet could have said it in prose, why should he take the immense trouble of saying it in verse?)

Of the letters themselves, Spender said:

> They are newsy and gossipily depressing… But except when he reminisces about his childhood or Swansea, they consist chiefly of the Thomas stereotype. The epistolary relationship with Watkins falls quickly into a scrounger-to-saint pattern and gets stuck there. The frankness is all of the over-boiled kind. Disappointing.

Vernon wondered whether Spender had actually read the letters, or was mixing them up with the stories in *Portrait of the Artist*, since there was no reminiscing about his childhood or Swansea in the book; but mostly he was indignant at the suggestion that Dylan was 'anything but the most generous of men'; and there was an exchange of short, sharp letters in the *Observer*, in the first of which Vernon wrote:

> I foresaw that lop-sided comment might be made on these

small items of borrowing, but I left them in. In their time and context they were significant, mattering so much to him, and not at all to me.

Although there were numerous reviews which commented on Dylan's borrowing from Vernon, this was the only one that he answered. He began to wonder whether it would, in fact, have been better to leave out all references to his small loans and gifts. It was a great relief for him to hear that Caitlin approved of their inclusion. She had sent him, on a postcard that was also a gramophone record, the following request:

> I wonder if you would be very kind and do me a great favour: to send me a copy of Dylan's letters, as I am only just nearly brave enough to glance at some of Dylan's stuff, which I could not bear within printed eyesight before, and I don't know where I can get it from in Italy.
>
> I did enjoy seeing you again after so long…bristling more than ever, were such a phenomenon feasible, with hedgehog integrity. Become more absolutely than was ever conceded to a much-married voluminous family man before, an abstract levitating sage. A pure, undespoiled, flying high above the squalor of roof tops visionary…
>
> Weathering the winter in Sicily is a dark hibernation of excessive light; hence my unnatural craving for literature.

Vernon was shocked that Dent had not sent Caitlin a copy of the book, and immediately sent one to her. She replied:

> Thank you very much for the book which I really do appreciate, and your excellent comments. But opening the pages of that early life makes it come back dreadfully near, like the day before yesterday, and my late life shrinks into putrid insignificance. So much for my great banging of doors with hollow echoes. I quite agree with you about leaving in all Dylan's money borrowings which are an essential part of the letters and make them more faultily touching.

Caitlin's approval was almost the only comfort that Vernon had that winter, as reviewers almost unanimously declared that the letters should not have been published. The *Tribune*, in a review headed *Stop the Dylan Craze*, said, "Mr Watkins has published a lot of trivial letters about trivial things, and it is a pity."

The *Yorkshire Post*, "joining," as it admitted, "in the expected chorus of disapproval", agreed with the *Tribune*.

> People antipathetic towards Dylan Thomas and his nest of cronies will probably derive a great deal of satisfaction from the publication of these letters; and even a critic well-disposed towards the poet and towards the printing of private correspondence generally, may feel a little taken aback by the trivia of much of the material here offered.

The nadir was reached in a review by Penelope Mortimer in the *Observer*. It is a triumph (or rather a disaster) of bad taste and ill-breeding, without the excuse of personal dislike to justify it since the lady knew neither Dylan nor Vernon.

> …I don't see any point in publishing these dreary letters, which only succeed in presenting him as a self-pitying, shiftless baby, who wouldn't do a thing for himself, some-one who lived such a trivial boring life that he sounds like a sort of cultured George Gambol.

John Davenport alone, in the *Spectator*, realised the value and the integrity of the letters.

> This book is justified by the astonishing unity of the material… But this is not a book of sloppy reminiscence, but a book really of technical reference. Pages 66 and 67… are a complete refutation of those who think Thomas did not know what he was saying or how best to say it. These are humble and illuminating pages. Nobody could be anything but the better for reading them, even if he were totally uninterested in poetry.

And there came words of praise from the *Mercure de France.*

> *Ce livre est précieux a plusieurs égards... Aussi ces lettres sont-elles un document indispensable sur la création artistique chez Thomas et sur la genèse de ses poemes.*

Vernon, while still convinced that the letters were 'the richest letters of our times', could hardly fail to be disappointed and depressed by their reception in England. But when the book came out in America in 1958, it was a very different matter. In every part of the United States it was received with acclamation by the critics, many of them distinguished poets themselves. Katherine Anne Porter, in the *New York Times Book Review*, expressed what most Americans seemed to feel about the spate of reminiscences which had poured out since Dylan's death.

> So many persons have looked at Dylan Thomas through themselves, it is a change for the better to have Thomas looking at himself through a friend, a good faithful gifted friend who played it straight. Here are no perverse sexual motives, no wifely jealousy and rivalry, no literary hangers-on elbowing each other out of the reflected glory, no wistful would-bes, hoping that a little of the genius would rub off on them if only they could get near enough. Oh, none of all that dreariness!

The book of letters was everywhere favourably compared to Brinnin's book and to Caitlin's *Leftover Life to Kill,* and was regarded by John Ciardi, in the *Saturday Review*, as restoring the picture of the dedicated poet.

> It is part of a Thomas pattern that the two biographies of him published to date have been more personal to the writers than to Thomas as the subject. John Malcolm Brinnin had been accused after Thomas's death by rumours as outrageous as they were baseless, and he unfortunately... seems to have been at least as much concerned to defend himself as to portray Thomas. Caitlin Thomas, following with her own intensely personal reactions... was certainly too close to the turmoil of Thomas's death for anything like a balanced portrait. With such cross-

motives at work it is small wonder to find that Thomas is lost in the shuffle, and inevitable that his more sensational antics should take over the writing. The letters to Vernon Watkins, close friend and admired fellow-poet, are most valuable as a first redressing of the balance.

The American critics seemed not only more alive to the wit, charm and real worth of the letters, but they had a far more sensitive insight into Dylan's life and character, and the compulsions which often drove him. R Phelps, in the *National Review*, commented on the 'zest and charm' which Thomas brought everywhere and to everyone.

There is even perhaps a clue here to the terrible question of why so bountiful a man was so little able to preserve himself, and died at thirty-nine. For in every one of these letters…there is the same inexhaustible wish to please. No matter what he is saying or how he feels… he is always turning somersaults, always striving to engage and delight, always exerting himself to be liked. This was his profoundest virtue – this need to take the trouble to reach others, but it was also his most debilitating weakness. Even a Welshman has only so much energy, and Dylan Thomas gave so great a proportion to the art of making himself loved that eventually there was none left for anything else, not even for keeping his body alive.

This is one of the most perceptive statements ever made about Dylan.

Chapter 15

BEHIND THE FABULOUS CURTAIN

I am not too proud to cry that He and he
Will never never go out of my mind. – D. T.

In December 1955, Vernon wrote to Francis:

Last month I went through Dylan's letters, copying them, because I found I had lost two or three… Then I was sent the manuscript notes of the poem Dylan was working on when he died: an elegy about his father's death. There were sixty pages of notes. I extended and completed a version of the poem from these, and this Spender is going to print in the February number of *Encounter*; do look for this, if it ever reaches your dark city.

He described, in a talk at Gregynog, in 1964, the actual labour of assembling the poem. He had promised, he said, that the talk should be about his own latest poems, the ones written or published since his book, *Affinities*, which came out in 1962.

But I shall begin by reading the very last poem which Dylan Thomas wrote. He left it unfinished. He had recited to me the opening lines in Swansea in 1953, and three years later I was handed all the manuscript work towards the poem, with a request that I should try to complete it. By a strange coincidence this work, in typescript and manuscript, and running to more than sixty pages, was handed to me on the very morning after I had spent more than a month copying his letters to me, a task which had occupied me most evenings until very late; so I had the advantage of having read Dylan's own writing continuously when I was asked to begin work on the poem. My first attempt failed. There were a great many versions and a great many variants. A week later I tried again, and the various jottings Dylan had made, consisting chiefly of single lines or a pair of lines, fell into shape. In the most complete versions, which were typed, it was clear that he had reached the 17th line, with a number of alternatives; and there was a nest of alterations and beginnings at that point. I was guided by the four prose notes he had made for the poem. Where two lines came together in the notebook drafts, I kept that order; but otherwise I did not respect at all the order of the pages.

The only word used in the whole poem without justification from the manuscript was 'plain' in line twenty-three, to rhyme with 'pain'. Of the added lines, sixteen were as Dylan wrote them, and the remainder were altered only by the inversion of one or two words. The provisional titles, *The Darkest Way*, *Too Proud to Die* and *True Death*, had been used in the preparatory drafts, but were rejected in favour of the title on the most complete. In his note in *Encounter*, Vernon wrote:

> In the third line I have chosen 'narrow pride' as against 'burning pride' although 'burning' occurs more often than 'narrow' in the transcripts; but it was 'narrow' in that line that he quoted to me from memory when I last saw him.

The order of the added lines might of course have been different, and the poem might, if Dylan had lived to write more lines, have been longer. But the completed poem, as it stands, is valid and moving. Dylan's death was the end of much that had been precious in Vernon's life, but it was not the end of everything that bound them. They were still engaged in poetry together. Before the death, Vernon had written very little prose; but now he was engaged with it to a degree that he would formerly have thought undesirable. He was continually asked for reviews, articles, forewords and other prose pieces; and though he refused many requests, he seldom turned down an opportunity to write about Dylan. He was, in any case, assembling a series of notes about Dylan for his own pleasure and use, incorporating everything he remembered about his friend. He could often draw on this material for reviews, but also the mere writing down of his memories would bring up other incidents forgotten until then.

J. A. Rolph had been compiling a bibliography of Dylan Thomas's work since 1952. Dylan had told Vernon about 'this fantastic project'; he would have thought it just as fantastic that his unmethodical friend should review such a professional – and in one sense unliterary – book as the bibliography. But Vernon made a surprisingly good job of it. His encyclopaedic memory for poetry and his loving recollection of almost every word Dylan ever said to him enabled him not only to appreciate but also to criticise such a meticulous production as that of Mr Rolph.

Future generations will not regard Dylan Thomas as a prolific writer. The exuberance and abundance associated with his work derived largely from his presence and conversation. The small number of his written books must be invisibly multiplied in the memories of those who knew him, for his company was itself a creative thing, releasing a stream of ideas. Yet he distrusted this exuberance, this leaping fountain of his imagination, and subjected it to the strictest control. Abundance which empties itself in work after work becomes purposeless without that arresting moment which examines the cause of its display; and it was this moment which interested Dylan Thomas: his obsession was with the motive force of nature, not with nature itself. With a loose, prolific writer the task of the bibliographer becomes prodigiously wide; meticulousness is brought to bear on the work which is not always justified by its extension, for critical work is outside the work of the bibliographer; he cannot emphasize what he admires or leave out what he does not like. His task is to complete the pattern of the work, and the degree of excitement in the pattern depends on its coherence. With some writers the pattern is not seen until its completion; with others it is lost in the process. In an ideal pattern everything has

Vernon after Dylan's death

value and the interest is not only sustained, but deepened, by the experience of life itself. In a supreme example, like Yeats or Beethoven, it is at once seen that the perseverance of the artist over a lifetime has enhanced the pattern and given to the last works an intensity made possible only by all that had gone before; yet even these works would not exist without the artist's willingness in absolute honesty and humility to start afresh.

After commenting on some omissions and details, which had escaped Mr Rolph's vigilance, Vernon allowed himself a crack at *Dylan Thomas in America*.

There is nothing irrelevant or misleading in the contents of this fine book. Those who feel that it is regrettable that the publishers use the dust-jacket to advertise the recent, and to this writer deplorable, book about Dylan Thomas's American tours, are able to discard it.

Vernon had always stuck to his decision never to review work by a living author, although reviewing would often have earned him money when he was hard up. Now that Dylan was dead, however, he did consent to review books by or about him, because he thought he knew, and would say, things other reviewers might not know or say. To Francis he wrote:

Dylan's book of broadcasts, *Quite Early One Morning*, is out, and I expect you have it. They are extraordinary, and most rich. The American one, which is being sent to me, is more complete, I believe, than the English one, which I reviewed for the *Times Literary Supplement*. I never do reviewing, though I've been asked to a lot lately, but I did review this.

It was a new experience for him, to study prose with care, even Dylan's prose. He came to respect it, and to see not only that it was closely related to the verse, but that it had its own unique value.

From his first beginnings, both in poetry and prose, Dylan Thomas had moved from a haunted, confused and symbol-charged shaping-place in the direction of the living voice... He never, however, lost his preoccupation with words, and it is doubtful whether any writer, cramming his work with life, joy and gaiety, has used words with greater cunning... The poetry was made by isolation, the prose by his social life, yet they acted upon each other, and out of this conflict came a new and miraculous use of language.

But always his own sense of the living Dylan and the tragedy of his death came upon him, even while celebrating his genius. It is impossible to close the book without regret, without an infinite sense of loss. Dylan Thomas as a broadcaster was unique. His place in sound radio was equivalent to Chaplin's place in the silent film. The depth and range of these talks is extraordinary, and extraordinary in its depth and subtle variations was the voice which gave them life.

Vernon always, when considering Dylan's prose, linked it to the poems. In a *T L S* review of *A Prospect of the Sea*, he commented on the early stories.

These four years (1934 to 1938) were intensely active ones for the poet. He used them to exercise and explore his imaginative powers, and to curb, as far as he could, their volcanic force, while his life moved from adolescence to maturity. The poems of *The Map of Love* testify to his triumph in that struggle, while the stories reveal the same imagination, but also the dust and heat. They are often directly linked with the poems, particular phrases like 'desireless familiar' in the story *The Orchards* which is found later in the poem *To Others Than You,* and in *Deaths and Entrances*, being common to both. They have, then, a particular significance as the quarry from which certain elements of the poems were drawn.

The same theme, of the relation of verse to prose, and of the relation of Dylan's nature to both, ran through an unpublished version of a foreword to *Adventures in the Skin Trade*.

In the stories of *Portrait of the Artist as a Young Dog,* he released the spring of bubbling life and comic invention which his friends had always known, though he had, until then, kept it out of his work. In *Adventures in the Skin Trade* the comic invention was directed against himself. He was a poet of tragic vision, but he was also a born clown, always falling naturally into situations which became ludicrous. Just as it is impossible to understand Lear without his Fool, it is impossible to have a clear picture of Dylan Thomas without the self-parody which appears in *Adventures in the Skin Trade*. It is a key, not only to something instantly recognised in his personality, but to something afterwards recognised in his tragedy and early death... Yet, like everything Dylan wrote, this intensely personal comedy was a part of him. This unique fragment, half fictional though it is, carries the unmistakeable stamp of his personality. It is real now because it was once real to him.

Vernon's last published comment on Dylan was a note for *Poetry* in 1961. It was called *Behind the Fabulous Curtain*. The title came from the last line of Dylan's poem *Today, This Insect and the World I Breathe:* 'My cross of tales behind the fabulous curtain'. It says, in its few short paragraphs, all that can truly be said of Dylan Thomas, and I give it in its entirety.

> It is difficult to explain to anyone who did not know Dylan Thomas why any study of him must remain totally inadequate. It is equally difficult to explain why those who knew him find themselves deeply handicapped in writing about him. The quality he prized most was seriousness, and he was a born clown, but was there any other poet of recent times who could create so quickly an intimacy of judgment, an apprehension of what was valid, in art and in life? That is perhaps one of the reasons why strangers who met him only once for a long conversation felt, after his death, that they had known him all their lives.

The entertainer and the intellectual alike were slightly ashamed after meeting him as he could beat them both at their own game, but if they were humble they quickly recognised that he was humble, too. The prig was his *bête noire*, the pedant a black-and-white crossword figure whom he didn't despise.

The variety of life and its abundance sang in his veins. He was born to praise it, and he did so most completely when war distorted it into every manifestation of horror. When the war ended, his own war continued. He was, on the one hand, enriched by the heroic comedy of people's lives, for he loved people, and, on the other, fascinated by artificial pattern, for the problems of form he had to solve in his last poems were subtle and more intricate than any he had ever set himself before. He found freedom in the late broadcast scripts, but pattern obsessed him. In this late work, the prose, with all its humorous invention, was made by his social life, the poetry by his isolation in spite of that, the isolation of the entertainer who has taken off his mask. A writer's mask can be fatal to him, and it is certain that the image the age demanded of Dylan Thomas was accelerated by his popularity. His infectious humour deceived everyone but himself. His method was not to retreat from the mask, but to advance beyond it, and in that exaggeration remain completely himself. He agreed readily with his detractors, and did not at all mind being misunderstood. Then, in the private dark, his exuberance was subjected to the strictest control. The public figure and the lyric poet whose work began and ended in the Garden of Eden came to terms, terms which no critic or friend has the complete equipment to analyse.

After the publication of the letters, Vernon was regarded as an expert commentator on Dylan's life and work. He became the often bewildered and always harassed target of hundreds of requests, varying from the simple, "I am doing a Master's thesis on Dylan Thomas. Any information will be welcome," to the more complex, "I am doing my Ph. D. on Dylan Thomas and enclose a 40-page questionnaire which I should like you to return immediately." These requests always came from America. English students in the early sixties were either more diffident or less enterprising than Americans, or had just not got around to realising that Dylan Thomas was the in-poet on whom to do a thesis. Sometimes, if their parents were rich or they had grants, the Americans came to Swansea. They descended on Vernon in the bank often enough for him to be taken off the counter, where the Americans, undeterred by growing queues of Welsh business-men vocally unsympathetic to scholarship, would go steadily through their 40-page lists of questions, carefully writing down each answer in longhand. Once, Vernon arrived home accompanied by a steel millionaire from Pittsburgh, bearing brandied peaches and Bourbon, and his young wife, who had begged that their wedding trip should include Wales, because she had once heard Dylan read poems. She tapped gamely about the rocky cliffs in her high heels (a gold bangle with her husband's name engraved on it jingled on one slender ankle) and took quantities of notes, while her husband looked fondly and proudly at her. He was not, he said, himself a literary man. They were staying at one of Swansea's oldest hotels, the Mackworth, which the millionaire said, not complainingly, had not the simple comfort of Claridge's.

University College, Swansea, asked Vernon to supervise the thesis of a French girl, who was attempting to study Dylan's poetry without any knowledge of Christianity or the Bible. Her parents were atheists and she had never been inside a church. Dylan's many Biblical allusions were completely lost on her, and all her scrupulous scholarship was of no use. She carefully annotated every reference, but would arrive for tutorial sessions vocal with frustration. "You say, we shall this week study *Marriage of a Virgin*, but 'ow can we study what 'as no sense? He say here, 'And the shipyards of Galilee's footprints 'ide a navy of doves.' Now I 'ave look up this Galilee, and it is a province in Northern Caesarea; what is to make of that?"

On Vernon's advice, she read the New Testament (because of the statement in Dylan's *Notes on the Art of Poetry* – "The story of the New Testament is part of my life."). But it made little impression on her, and she could not see why it should have so strongly influenced Dylan that he must make such frequent reference to it. "No," she said stoutly. "In my opinion, this is a poet which look for the difficulty."

Many critics were saying the same thing. Explicating Dylan Thomas had, by the early sixties, become an industry. But the charge that (at least after some of the early poems) Dylan was deliberately obscure could always rouse Vernon to greater fury than any attack on his own poetry. He would enter the lists of any controversy on this subject; a letter to the *Spectator* in September 1964 is typical of many.

> It is not always easy to shift an argument about a poet to a true level of enquiry, as the combatants forget that it is the poetry that matters, not what they say about it. Yet the old charge that Dylan intended to baffle and confuse his readers is not quite dead.
>
> By the time he was thirty Dylan Thomas had acquired a mastery of the suggestive power of words unequalled perhaps by any of his contemporaries. He was also very resourceful, and he would use all the mechanics of composition, which he often called tricks, to serve his imagination; yet without accident or luck, that element which gives permanence to a work of art, he never found them completely satisfying.
>
> Had he trusted obscurity, he could have been much more obscure, and had he trusted the exploitation of language alone, the body of his finished poetry would have been much greater than it is. He trusted, finally, what lay beyond mere mechanics, and so was able to coordinate and transcend them. He was extremely patient in his search for what he wanted in order to match the need of his imagination...
>
> The leap from the persuasive word to the unalterable one is usually abrupt, and nothing is proved by Robert Frost's study of a manuscript of Dylan Thomas where the rhyming

mechanics for a poem were set down. To be left behind with these mechanics is an incomplete situation.

The purpose of all revision is to arrive at lucidity without loss of content, and if the work becomes more intricate in the process, this only means that the intricacy was already there, but its expression was not. Just as a poet can only be partially understood in his lifetime, he may well be misunderstood after his death. Dylan Thomas did not mind being misunderstood, but anyone who thinks he aimed at baffling people or at obscure utterance, or approached poetry with anything but complete honesty, is more deeply mistaken than he knows.

When David Holbrook's book *Llareggub Revisited* came out in 1962, Vernon read it with mounting irritation. It seemed to him simply perverse. He began to annotate it, but gave up in despair. "To do the job properly, I should have to write a paragraph for every sentence of Holbrook's," he said. It seems likely that at one time he intended to write at least an article about it, since he left a sheaf of notes containing a detailed refutation of many of Holbrook's contentions. These notes contain a final section evidently intended to demolish the claims of many critics to assess Dylan's work. It begins:

Handicaps of the Author in common with most of Dylan's critics

1) Did not know the man.

2) Has been misled by the legend of Dylan Thomas built up by those who did not know him.

3) Begins with a false hypothesis that Dylan Thomas was an arrogant eccentric enfant terrible. This was one of Dylan's masks, but it is one that he discarded in writing serious poetry.

The idea of writing a book about Dylan and his work, always rejected before reading Holbrook's book, was afterwards never entirely abandoned. Vernon continued to add to the pile of Notes on Dylan Thomas, and, indeed, the last addition to them was jotted down on the train going through the Rocky Mountains, three weeks before his own death. It was scribbled on a Canadian Pacific envelope (on the front of which is a note that a grizzly bear has just been sighted) and it says:

> *Dylan.* His revolt at plundered innocence. His mastery, both in verse and prose, of the suggestive power of words. The pivotal, organic word forking two meanings in the context, the second proliferating in the imagination from the first; e. g. 'And dig your grave in my breast.' This device is used in the later, more lyrical poetry.

Probably Vernon thought that the retirement he did not live to enjoy would give him the leisure he had never had to write a book of prose. Meanwhile, a great many other people, who were in fact writing books about Dylan, came or wrote to him, always seeking the help which he readily gave. They often wanted photographs, too, which he as readily lent. Bill Read came to Pennard in the autumn of 1963, to look for material for his book, *The Days of Dylan Thomas,* which Vernon gave him in abundance, and which he acknowledged by writing:

> I don't know how to thank you properly for all your generosity and kindness in helping me prepare the book... I think I have followed your various comments to me exactly – at least I have intended to. If you should note any error of fact or interpretation I would be very grateful if you would let me know.

Ralph Maud sent a copy of *Entrances to Dylan Thomas' Poetry,* inscribed: 'To Vernon Watkins, with thanks for his invaluable Letters.' William Moynihan inscribed *The Craft and Art of Dylan Thomas,* 'To Vernon Watkins: in greatest admiration of the poet and the man and in appreciation of kindnesses.'

Vernon also helped Dr B. W. Murphy, an American psychiatrist, with his thesis on Dylan, in which he analysed the creative and destructive content in Dylan's work. Constantine FitzGibbon sent the typescript of *The Life of Dylan Thomas* to be vetted before being sent to the publishers. Vernon sent him back fifteen foolscap pages of single-spaced typing containing corrections, additions, emendations, and suggestions, most of which proved to be of use.

Constantine later consulted Vernon about the selection of Dylan's letters that was to come out in 1966. Vernon had some correspondence with Lady Snow (Pamela Hansford Johnson), about some of the early letters, in the course of which she wrote:

> (Constantine) seems to have made his selection with humanity and I am sure he will delete what is really hurtful... Dylan was often extremely unpleasant about his mother, whom he loved and whom I loved. It is true that my mother was pretty bored with her when they first met, since Dylan and I were off to Gower all day, and the mothers had nothing to do but sit and chat... You are the one person of whom I never heard Dylan speak with anything but affection.

It was not only from America that the writers on Dylan came; by the sixties his fame had penetrated to the rest of Europe and further afield. Georges-Albert Astre had an article on Dylan in *Les Lettres Françaises* in January 1963, together with some of the letters to Vernon; to whom, also, the notes on Dylan in *La Poésie Anglaise* owed much. His copy is inscribed, "*Avec ma gratitude, et mon amical souvenir.*" *Bajo el Bosque de Leche* is inscribed by one of its translators, "*con agradacimiento, admiracion y afecto.*" It seems, after all, as though Vernon had written his book on Dylan, through many proxies. Only none of them was the book he himself would have written.

In 1960, Roberto Sanesi's book, *Dylan Thomas*, was published in Milan. Vernon had met the young Sanesi soon after Dylan's death, and he became a close friend. Sanesi met Ceri Richards, and a long and fruitful association developed. Both Dylan and Vernon had presented the artist with many themes from their poems, and in 1954 he had held an exhibition, *Homage to Two Poets*, at the Glyn Vivian Art Gallery in Swansea. Sanesi translated poems by both poets, and eventually published a book on Vernon's early poetry, *Taliesin a Gower*. Ceri did a series of sketches based on Vernon's translations of Sanesi's poems. All three collaborated on *Elegiac Sonnet*, published in the *Imaggini e Testi* Series by M'Arte Edizioni, Milano, 1970. This consists of two lithographs by Ceri Richards on a poem by Vernon, translated into Italian by Sanesi.

> Over this universal grass the sky
> Brings to the grieving earth its great reward,
> And it was right to lay ambition by,
> The strongest will being deep and the way hard.
> The body sleeping where the dead leaves lie
> Gives back to trees from colours they discard
> The patient light of its own penury
> Out of whose silence wakes the living word.
> And we who wake, who saw the swallows' wings
> Seeking the turning-point of their own cloud,
> Draw to one place his love of vanished things.
> It is not this that leaves the heart's way ploughed;,
> It is the shade the sun no longer flings
> Of one who touched the humble and the proud.

It was also because of Dylan that Vernon found himself contributing to scholarly reference books. In 1963 Rainbird, Maclean brought out *The Concise Encyclopaedia of English and American Poets and Poetry,* with Stephen Spender and Donald Hall as Editors. Spender wrote that he wished, "To make this book representative of the best contemporary thought about poetry by the greatest living scholars, critics and poets." Vernon said, on receiving this letter, that he instantly thought of Molière's *Que diable allait -il faire dans cette galère,* but he set to work to summarize his thoughts about Dylan in the 70 words allowed. Again, as in the *Times* obituary, his contribution was quite unlike anyone else's.

> From the first, he set himself the task of remaking the language in terms of his own vision. His first book... revealed an idiom, new to English poetry, whose concentrated force was easily adapted to the correspondence he sought between sexual imagery and themes of vast metaphysical range. The stubborn originality of his verse derived from a singleness of vision, at once Freudian and Biblical, which remained fresh throughout

his life, as though his eyes still remembered the Garden of Eden.

After Dylan's death, the references in Vernon's lectures or poetry readings became even more frequent than they had been during his lifetime. His address to the Poetry Society in 1966 is typical.

> I have not time to talk about the extremely rich and searching imagination of Dylan himself. His poetry is *ancient*, as it is always dealing with first and last things. I remember acknowledging my great debt to him at Oxford in 1952. I had… stated my belief that a true style can never be learned from a contemporary, and a poet can only really relate himself to ancient and dead poets, and be influenced by them. At the end I was challenged. I was asked to reconcile this statement to my other one about the profound influence of Dylan Thomas. I said, "Dylan Thomas *is* an ancient poet. He happens to be alive." This can no longer be said, but his work proclaims it.

Vernon's first visit to America came about entirely through Dylan's intervention. In New York, in 1950, Dylan had first met Theodore Roethke, whose poems he and Vernon admired greatly. Dylan read Roethke some of Vernon's poems, which Roethke liked very much. Years later, when he was Professor of Poetry at Washington University, Seattle, and was leaving for a sabbatical year, he asked Vernon to replace him. At that time, Vernon was neither able nor willing to go to America, but Roethke's recommendation to the Chairman of the English Department was so strong that, after his death, Vernon was persuaded to become Visiting Professor of Poetry in Seattle. He commemorated both Dylan and Roethke in his poem *At Cwmrhydyceirw Quarry*.

> Yet grooves unwind voices, and he who engraves
> This stone, soon in his childhood park to lie,
> Shall cut lines incised like a breaking cry,
> And give to stone that undulant line of waves.
> But who had guessed, in the hush of many graves
> Riven by love, it was Roethke's turn to die?

The meeting of Dylan with Roethke in Seattle was in his mind only a week before his own death, when he wrote the light poem, *Arrival in East Shelby*, which includes the verse

> But what a stir and what a rumpus
> Ran from the station round the campus
> When Thomas, finger stuck in bottle,
> Taxied to Roethke in Seattle.

It was in Cwmrhydyceirw Quarry that Vernon and the sculptor Ronald Cour found the blue pennant stone which now stands in Cwmdonkin Park in memory of Dylan. In January 1963 Vernon wrote to Francis:

> Tomorrow a television man is coming down from Bristol or Cardiff, and he will take me to Dylan's house or Cwmdonkin Park, and ask about the absence of a memorial to Dylan in Swansea. Dylan hated ostentatious things, but a lot of people coming from all over the world have marvelled that there is nothing to show that he was born and lived here. Some lines, perhaps, will be carved, some lines from one of the poems and perhaps set, unobtrusively in Cwmdonkin Park, but I don't know when.

The 'television man' interviewed Vernon standing rather forlornly in Cwmdonkin Drive, in the drifting snowflakes of a January dusk. He was cold from standing about, and his plea for some memorial to Swansea's famous son was not as impassioned as it might have been, but the programme had some important repercussions. A report of it reached New York, and, on the first of February, a cablegram was delivered to him at the bank, addressed only to Vernon Watkins, Swansea. Its text was as follows:

> Please allow us consider financing plaque honouring Dylan Thomas. Can you ascertain costs and write Caedmon Records.

Vernon immediately wrote to David Jones to ask whether he would consider doing the lettering on any stone that might be thought suitable, and received on February 2 the following answer:

> About Dylan's thing: I think you had better rule me out, for I am not a letter-cutter in either stone or wood... What I would suggest is that you or whoever is responsible get a good letter-cutter to do this thing *Er cof am Dylan*. I think it ought to have a bit of Welsh in it, if only that bit in place of *In Memoriam*.

After interviews with Swansea officials, Vernon wrote to tell the two ladies who ran Caedmon Records, Barbara Holdridge and Marianne Mantell, that the Town Council had given permission for a stone to be set up in Cwmdonkin Park. Mrs. Holdridge answered:

> I cannot tell you how much pleasure it would give the two of us... to help in some way the perpetuation of Dylan's name. It is now eleven years since we first met him. In that time we have done everything possible to ensure the continuity of his voice in our world. If we can now do something else, to pay in some small measure our debt to Dylan as friend and poet, we shall be grateful. The plaque in Cwmdonkin Park is a sensitive and good thought. We hope that you will have it executed to your satisfaction, for we know that it will then be as we too would wish it. If the cost is not above fifty pounds, please don't hesitate to go ahead, and have us billed. If more is involved, we'll need to decide whether we can pay the extra amount also. I hope that this happens. It would be such a good way to begin the year.

It did happen, but it took time, in spite of all that Vernon and Ronald Cour could do. But, by September, Vernon was able to write that the dedication of the stone would take place on the anniversary of Dylan's death; and Mrs. Holdridge wrote:

> We did wonder whether the Dylan project was in the working stages, and we are very happy to know that it is now so nearly done... The simple stone memorial you have described pleases us very much, and we look forward to having a photograph of it beside the water... Knowing how much this memorial

means to you, it would not be right for us to thank you for making it possible; but perhaps you will allow us to thank you for allowing us to have a small part in its fulfilment.

After the dedication, Vernon sent the ladies a photograph. It showed the water and the trees in Cwmdonkin Park, and between them the stone that was for many years to be Swansea's only memorial to its poet son – set there, not by Swansea, but by America.

In January 1968, *Poetry (Chicago)* carried on the inside of its cover the words: "VERNON WATKINS 1906 – 1967," and the editorial comment, "We learn with shock and sorrow, just as this issue goes into galley-proof, of the sudden death of Vernon Watkins."

In the same issue appeared the poem *Cwmrhydyceirw Elegiacs*, which shows that the stone in that Swansea park, and the quarry of its birth, were still in Vernon's mind a few months before his own death. It is safe to say that, to the end of his own life, the thought of Dylan was never out of Vernon's mind or heart.

In the last eighteen months of his life, Vernon was still occupied with Dylan's unfinished verse. In a broadcast talk produced by Douglas Cleverdon in September 1950, Dylan had explained that the three poems, *In Country Sleep, Over Sir John's Hill* and *In the White Giant's Thigh* were part of a long sequence to be called *In Country Heaven*. A fragmentary version of this was sent to Vernon in 1955; but a much more resolved version, consisting of eight complete stanzas and three lines, was sent to him in 1966 by William Moynihan. On this foundation Vernon improvised, 'with no manuscript justification at all', another five stanzas and two lines. It is a remarkable achievement.

Vernon sailed for America in September 1967, to teach a course in Modern Poetry at the University of Washington in Seattle. But he lived only two weeks after his arrival. His ashes were brought back to Pennard, and in St. Mary's church there is a memorial which bears the words the one poet had written in memory of the other:

> Death cannot steal the light which love has kindled,
> Nor the years change it.

AFTERWORD

I hold from heaven the power to see what's gone
So clearly, that what is or is to be
Hinders no whit the noblest I have known,
His passion rooted, singing like a tree. – V W.

Very few obituaries of Dylan Thomas made any mention of Vernon Watkins. Every obituary of Vernon that I have seen mentions Dylan, often to compare their poetry. Philip Larkin said in the *Times*:

> He always stressed an affinity with his friend Dylan Thomas... Where Thomas was strongly wrought, earthy and even humorous in his poems, however, Watkins was abstract, rhapsodic and light in texture.

The *South Wales Evening Post* said:

> To few towns has befallen the honour of nurturing two poets of world-acknowledged eminence in the same generation. The friendship of Dylan Thomas and Vernon Watkins in pre-war Swansea is one of the most famous of literary affinities. Neither owed any measure of his fame to the other, but both benefited by their exchange of ideas on poetry... Yet their temperaments and ways of life were very different – Dylan the exhibitionist, bohemian and improvident; Vernon the quiet-living bank clerk, respected by all who knew him: Dylan burnt out at 40, Vernon, though eight years his senior, surviving him by 14 years during which his mystical thought deepened, his fame steadily grew, and his devotion to Dylan's memory never waned.

In the book, *Vernon Watkins 1906- 1967*, edited by Leslie Norris, and containing tributes in prose and verse, twelve of the eighteen contributors mention Dylan, but not one attempts any assessment of the friendship. Hugo Williams remembered the unassuming way he assumed himself to be of interest – in long, hilarious, passenger-seat monologues – solely for his friendship with the ever- present 'Dylan.' And this was an impression Vernon also gave his colleagues at the University of Washington; that his sole justification for being there was that he had known Dylan Thomas. Already in his lifetime, the myth had arisen that Vernon represented a stable element in Dylan's unstable world. Dr B. W. Murphy, in his thesis, *Creation and Destruction: Notes on Dylan Thomas*, wrote about their relationship:

> It is timely to state how important Watkins was to Dylan, who depended on him in several ways. I believe Vernon was the ideal father of Dylan's family romance, and without his influence it seems likely to me that Thomas would not have developed personally and poetically as he did, and may (sic) have disintegrated much earlier.

And in the memorial volume, Glyn Jones commented on the fact that Vernon was prepared to endure forty years of routine to be able to concentrate on poetry.

> This sort of thorough-going renunciation Dylan, although himself incapable of any such single-mindedness, could understand and esteem, perhaps even revere. It is easy to see why he placed so much trust in Vernon and leaned so heavily upon him. In the mounting disorder of Dylan's affairs the serene dedication and the Christian acceptance of Vernon must have seemed like a still centre, a point of unattainable sanity.

I would give a great deal if Vernon and Dylan could have returned from the Afterworld for one short hour, to read these remarkable statements; to hear their roars of coarse laughter, to hear Vernon saying, "This is another fine myth you've got me into." But, indeed, such claims do not have the status of a myth; they are simply gigantic blunders, colossal mistakes. It cannot be too strongly emphasised that they are simply *wrong.* Dylan had no 'family romance', and did not in the least want an 'ideal father'. His own father was strict and repressive, but he loved Dylan, and Dylan loved him, and certainly wanted no substitute. And as for the 'serene dedication' and 'Christian acceptance' of working in a bank, Dylan thought nothing of it. He knew that Vernon had to support himself, and was quite incapable of writing stories or articles for a living, as he himself did; just as he was incapable of working in a bank. That was how things were, and Dylan accepted his own kind of life just as Vernon accepted his.

Far from leaning heavily on Vernon, he considered himself the more practical one of the two (and perhaps he was, marginally). During the war, he shepherded Vernon about in London pubs and clubs with great assurance, where they both left their possessions indiscriminately. He certainly respected Vernon as a poet, though I believe he thought (rightly) that he was years behind Dylan himself in poetic maturity. He loved discussing poetry seriously with Vernon, and this was possibly something that he missed after he had left Swansea; I doubt whether he ever met another poet prepared to spend infinite time on the craft that was the real meaning of life to them both. It was also a bonus that Vernon would type his poems and lend, or give, him money when he was in need. 'The mounting disorder of his affairs' was simply that he spent more money than he earned. I don't think he would ever have abandoned Caitlin and his children for either of the American women, nor would he have lived permanently anywhere but Wales. He liked swaggering about in London, but Wales was where he felt comfortable, and Swansea where his heart was.

Constantine FitzGibbon, who was a close friend of Vernon's, perpetuated another myth in *The Life of Dylan Thomas.*

> His friendship with Vernon Watkins was perhaps, from the point of view of the poet, the most important of his life after Dan Jones's... His relationship with Vernon Watkins was henceforth to be close and special... He provided the Welsh counterpoint to Dylan's roaring London friendships, but did so with an ease

and flavour that Dylan's more provincial Welsh friends, such as Dan Jones, lacked.

But, in fact, Vernon, though he had been educated in England, had never completed his degree course, whereas Dan had written a Doctoral thesis and had also spent years living abroad; but Vernon had only spent holidays abroad. Dan had also read much more in various languages than Vernon, who read only poetry, and was more sophisticated in every way. But Dylan didn't particularly like sophistication; he liked Vernon and Dan because they were Welsh boys at heart, and he was at ease with them. It is true that Vernon introduced Dylan to many foreign poets, such as Rilke, Lorca, Malherbe and others, but Dylan liked hearing poetry, and never thought of it as being provincial or otherwise.

So the picture of Dylan's and Vernon's friendship seems to me to be slanted in all sorts of ways. One thing that seems to me to have been entirely neglected is that they both had exactly the same sense of humour, and were both very witty men. They liked all sorts of humour; their favourite films were those of Chaplin, Laurel and Hardy and the Marx Brothers.

Part of Dylan's early fooling about in London pubs, I believe, came from his passion for these films. When Harpo Marx bit a girl's leg, or advanced on her buttons, eyes gleaming, Dylan thought it hysterically funny; he did not always understand why no-one thought so when he did it. It took him some years to realise the difference.

But Vernon and he also liked more sophisticated humour, such as Beachcomber and Timothy Shy. Word-play was a part of Dylan's life, as one can see even in his late letters, and it was a substantial part of his friendship with Vernon, who would always appreciate and respond appropriately. But in the end, Dylan was a child of the Muse; his real life was in words, and especially in verse. Friends might come and go; he liked them and wanted them for money, company, help of all sorts, but he did not need them, and made little or no effort to see them. It was always they who had to make the effort to see him. It is ridiculous to speak of any of them influencing him in any way: as C. S. Lewis said of

Charles Williams, "You might as well try to influence a bandersnatch."

Vernon knew from the first day he met Dylan that he had been given the inestimable privilege of knowing a genius, and he realised that he must guard and help this genius in any way he could. I think he regarded himself as an elder brother who must protect and take every care possible of this brilliant and cherished younger brother; he was always anxious about his well-being when Dylan moved out of his ken. Their great similarity was that both of them might have said with Milton about the Muse and Love, "Both them I serve, and of their train am I." Like all her servants, however social their lives, however deeply they loved their families and friends, they were at heart solitaries; for each, his true life was spent in 'those hours / For which the heart must wait', listening for the right words and making their poems. And after all, it is the poetry which greatly and deeply affects us; the lives of poets are interesting to us only because of that.

Beethoven said to a critic speaking disparagingly of great musicians, "Honour Mozart and Haydn by not mentioning their names." If you can't speak with respect of the great dead, it is better not to speak of them at all. By all means, tell the truth about them (if you are sure it *is* the truth), but honour their work. Those who have no reverence or compassion for Dylan Thomas (and I am thinking of a recent biography and a television programme) would do better not to speak of him at all.

INDEX

Index

For a full list of Lolfa publications
– including David Thomas' *The Dylan Thomas Trail* –
send now for our new, free, full-colour Catalogue
or you may surf into our website
www.ylolfa.com
and order books on-line.

Talybont Ceredigion Cymru/*Wales* SY24 5AP
01970 832 304
ylolfa@ylolfa.com
www.ylolfa.com